At Home with the Presidents

Judditive Morris

John Wiley & Sons, Inc.
New York • Chichester • Weinheim • Brisbane • Singapore • Toronto

For my son, Christopher, again, and for the women of my family and my extended family: Addye Mae Sellers, Vada Hart Webb, Martha Webb, Claudia Betti, Dora MacKay, Jan James, Juddi Boyce, Kerry Perkins Morris, Marty James, Ginger James, Lauren Boyce, Leila Bower Boullion, Antonella Betti, Terry Webb, Linda Perkins, Barbara Perkins, and Frances Quezada (Mija).

All images are courtesy of the Library of Congress, Prints and Photographs Division, except for:

Page 6, Mount Vernon Ladies Association; page 8, National Park Service, Adams National Historic Site; page 19, National Trust for Historic Preservation, Montpelier, photo by Philip Beaurline; page 23, Ash Lawn-Highland, Charlottesville, VA; page 29, The Hermitage, Nashville, TN; page 35, Department of the Interior, National Park Service, Martin Van Buren Historic Site; page 39, Berkeley Plantation; page 43, Sherwood Forest Plantation, Charles City, VA, photo by Greg Hadley; page 47, James K. Polk Home, Columbia, TN; page 51, National Cemetery System, Department of Veterans Affairs; pages 56 and 58, Phelps of Hillsboro, 35 Main Street, Box 921, Hillsborough, NH 03244; page 61, The Foundation for the Preservation of Wheatland; page 65, Lincoln Home National Historic Site; page 67, Andrew Johnson NHS, National Park Service; pages 71 and 75, National Park Service—Manhattan Sites; page 77, Rutherford B. Hayes Presidential Center, Fremont, OH, photo by Gilbert Gonzalez; pages 79 and 81, James A. Garfield II; pages 83 and 85, The President Chester A. Arthur State Historic Site, Vermont Division for Historic Preservation; page 93, President Benjamin Harrison Home Foundation; page 97, Stark County Historical Society, Canton, OH; page 102, Sagamore Hill National Historic Site, National Park Service; pages 104 and 106, William Howard Taft National Historic Site; pages 108 and 110, Woodrow Wilson Birthplace & Museum, Staunton, VA; page 116, National Baseball Hall of Fame Library, Cooperstown, NY; page 118, Vermont Division for Historic Preservation, President Calvin Coolidge State Historic Site, photo by Frank L. Forward; pages 120 and 122, Herbert Hoover Presidential Library-Museum, National Historic Site, West Branch, IA; page 127, Franklin Delano Roosevelt Library; pages 129 and 131, Harry S. Truman Library; page 133, Dwight D. Eisenhower Library; page 135, Eisenhower Center, Abilene, KS; pages 137 and 139, John F. Kennedy Library, Boston; page 141, Lyndon Baines Johnson Library, photo by Arnold Newman; page 144, Lyndon Baines Johnson Library, photo by Frank Wolfe; pages 146 and 149, Richard Nixon Library and Birthplace, Yorba Linda, CA; pages 151 and 153, Gerald R. Ford Library and Museum, Grand Rapids, MI; page 157, Jimmy Carter Library, photo by David Stanhope; pages 159 and 161, Ronald Reagan Library; page 163, George Bush Presidential Library and Museum; page 165, George Bush Presidential Library and Museum, photo by F. Carter Smith; page 170, Clinton Birthplace Foundation, photo by Wanda Powell.

This book is printed on acid-free paper. ♾

Published by John Wiley & Sons, Inc.
Published simultaneously in Canada.

Design and production by Navta Associates, Inc.

Library of Congress Cataloging-in-Publication Data:
Morris, Juddi.
At home with the presidents / Juddi Morris.
p. cm.
Includes bibliographical references.
Summary: Describes the lives of the presidents of the United States, their families, and the various homes, libraries and other sites associated with each.
ISBN 0-471-13773-1 (alk. paper)
1. Presidents—United States—Homes and haunts—Juvenile literature. 2. Presidents—United States—Biography—Miscellanea—Juvenile literature. 3. Historic sites—United States—Juvenile literature. [1. Presidents. 2. Presidents—Homes and haunts.]
I. Title.
E176. 1.M88 1999 98-54096
973—dc21

10 9 8 7 6 5 4 3 2 1

Contents

Introduction

History springs to life in the birthplaces, homes, and libraries of the U.S. presidents. After a visit to these historic sites, you have a better picture of the men who have led our country. We learn that our forty-one chief executives were people much like ourselves. They had problems and faults, tragedies and joys, successes and failures, just as we do. In fact, it has been said that they were "just ordinary men in extraordinary times."

The one dwelling they've almost all had in common is the White House, originally called the President's Mansion, which has served as the home of every U.S. president since John Adams. Each of the presidents has left an imprint on 1600 Pennsylvania Avenue.

Before the White House was built, everybody had ideas about who should design the building and what it should look like, but no one could agree. Finally, Thomas Jefferson suggested holding a contest to see which architect could come up with the best plan. Within a few months, nine entries came in, and an Irish American from South Carolina, James Hoban, won the competition.

Hoban's plan was chosen because it was simple and didn't look like a palace. Most of the other entries were much too grand. One entry even had a large throne room! But Hoban's design fit the nation's idea of itself—simple yet large enough to qualify as the most important house in the nation.

John Adams and his family were the first to live in the still unfinished house. In a letter to her daughter, Abigail Adams complained about the place. She hated the wet plaster and the barnlike feeling of the building. During Thomas Jefferson's time at the White House, he added low wings to the east and west. James Monroe added the rounded portico (porch) on the south, and Andrew Jackson added a rectangular portico on the north.

But by the 1940s, people did not want the outside of the White House tampered with in any way. When Harry Truman added a second floor to the South Portico, to replace the sun awnings that had become soiled and torn, he had a battle on his hands.

The inside of the great house has been altered in some way by every family that has lived there. In the early days, walls were ripped out to accommodate gas pipes, electric wires, bathrooms, and elevators. Furnishings have been changed as presidents have come and gone. It has been said that Eleanor Roosevelt, who lived in the White House longer than any other First Lady, made fewer changes to the interior than any other president's wife. She preferred to concentrate her time and energy on causes, not fabric samples!

Although the White House remains in very good condition, some of the presidential birthplaces and homes have fallen into disrepair through the years; some have been destroyed by fire, torn down, or sold to private citizens. Most, however, have been restored or preserved as historic sites. They range from the Hermitage, which looks as magnificent as it did in Andrew Jackson's time, to the tidy frame house of Millard Fillmore.

Mount Vernon was the first presidential home to be preserved. In 1853, driving past the residence in her carriage, Miss Ann Pamela Cunningham was shocked to see how shabby the place looked. She set to work and organized the Mount Vernon Ladies Association to restore George Washington's estate to its original glory.

Since then twenty-nine nonprofit historical organizations have been formed to preserve other presidential sites. Today, the National Park Service administers more than twenty presidential birthplaces or homes.

The system of presidential libraries, first established by Franklin Roosevelt to protect his valuable documents, is overseen by the National Archives and Records Administration. This agency supervises the libraries of Presidents Hoover, Franklin Roosevelt, Truman, Eisenhower, Kennedy, Johnson, Ford, Carter, Reagan, and Bush. (The Hayes and Nixon libraries are administered privately.)

While these libraries are usually reserved for the use of scholars and historians, their museum sections are open to the general public. Through exhibits, artifacts, and audiovisual programs, they are wonderful places to get to know the presidents of the United States.

George Washington

George Washington, our first president, is known as the "father of his country." As the commander in chief of the colonial forces during the Revolution, he led the struggle for American independence. In doing so, he became a hero and was elected president by unanimous vote. It was largely through his leadership as president that the thirteen colonies became a nation. In fact, Washington was admired so much that some people wanted to crown him king of America and call his wife Lady Martha.

"A Gentleman Should Never Curse"

George was born on February 22, 1732, at Pope's Creek, Virginia. His father, who was active in community affairs, owned a large farm where he grew tobacco. Little is known of George's early life, but we do know that he had three younger brothers and a younger sister, as well as two older half brothers from his father's first marriage.

Early on, he showed a gift for mathematics and surveying (measuring land). He also was an excellent horseman. George was not a great reader, but he was very conscious that he must grow up to be a gentleman. He found a book that listed 110 "Rules of Civility." He copied down all these rules of gentlemanly behavior, which included

"A gentleman should never curse or brag" and "A gentleman should not pry into other people's business."

When George was eleven, his father died, leaving several farms to his sons. Lawrence, one of George's half brothers, inherited the land on which he later built Mount Vernon. George adored his older brother and spent as much time as possible with him, but George's mother was jealous of the two brothers' relationship and tried to keep the younger boy at home. Mrs. Washington was very possessive, even though she seemed to disapprove of almost everything George did. When George wanted to join the British Navy, his mother forbade it. All his life, George tried to be a dutiful son, but Mary Ball Washington often accused him of neglect and scolded him constantly. Even after he became the first president of the United States, she did not acknowledge the importance of her son's achievements.

Two Horses Were Shot from Under Him

Since he could not get permission to join the navy, he began to work as a land surveyor. When Lawrence unexpectedly died, the heartbroken George inherited Mount Vernon.

At 6 foot 2, George was considered very large for those days and seemed even taller because of his good posture. George joined the Virginia home army and fought in the French and Indian War, in which France and Native American warriors banded together to fight against Great Britain and the American colonists. George became an aide to General Braddock, and in one battle, two horses were shot from under him and four bullets ripped through his coat.

He made the rank of colonel before the war was over. During this time he met an attractive widow named Martha Custis, who had two young children. George and Martha fell in love, married, and settled at

Fact or Fiction?

Through the years much misinformation has been published about George Washington's life. He did not chop down his father's cherry tree. That story was invented by Mason Weems, a popular writer of the time. It has also been said that Washington wore a wig. He did not. He wore his hair tied back, military fashion, in a queue, or small tail, and powdered it in the style of the time. And did he have wooden teeth? No, but he had several sets of false teeth made from gold, lead, and ivory. It is said that he even had sets made of sheep, cow, and hippopotamus teeth. Unfortunately none of them fit well and they always caused him discomfort.

Mount Vernon. They attended parties and fox hunts and entertained houseguests, who sometimes stayed for weeks at a time. Both Martha and George loved to dance, and they also enjoyed concerts and plays. Their only sadness was that they could have no children of their own, but George was devoted to his stepchildren.

It Was a Long and Bloody War

Washington was elected to the Virginia House of Burgesses (the equivalent of a modern state legislature), where he was an effective but quiet member. But times were hard and the colonists were suffering under the rule of King George III of England. They had to buy goods from England that were expensive and poorly made and were required to sell their crops to the English at low prices. To make matters worse, England tried to force the American colonists to pay higher taxes.

To discuss these problems, Washington joined other colonial leaders in Philadelphia for what was called the First Continental Congress. The delegates told England of their concerns, but they were ignored. In 1775, war with England had started and the American Revolution was under way. The colonists formed an American Continental Army. John Adams proposed George Washington as the commander in chief, and he was unanimously selected by the Congress.

George Washington—Firefighter?

George Washington might have had a very different career, for he was an enthusiastic firefighter. He began running to fires and helping to put them out when he was a child and continued until just a few months before his death, when he fought a blaze in Alexandria, Virginia.

It was a long and bloody war, but the colonial army prevailed and in 1781 the British surrendered. Although it was a happy day, it was a sorrowful time for George and Martha, for her son and daughter had died during the long siege.

Washington Dreaded the Responsibility

Washington resigned as commander of the army and returned home to Mount Vernon, where he hoped to live peaceably the rest of his life. He was not there for long. In 1787 he was called back to Philadelphia to lead the Constitutional Convention. During the four months the convention met, the delegates wrote the Constitution of the United States.

On April 6, 1789, George Washington was elected president. He took the oath of office on April 30, 1789, on a balcony of Federal Hall in New York City, then the capital of the United States. As he took the oath of office, Washington spontaneously added the words "so help me

God," and kissed the Bible. A modest man, Washington dreaded the responsibility of forming a new government, fearing that he might not be equal to the job. Once elected, though, he moved ahead decisively.

George Washington was reelected in 1792 but rejected a third term. He could hardly wait to get back to Mount Vernon, for he considered himself a farmer above all and was happiest on his land. He returned home in 1797, but he lived only two more years. After riding his horse through a snowstorm, Washington caught a cold. His throat became infected and on December 14, 1799, he died at the age of sixty-seven.

☆ Visit ☆ Mount Vernon

Today, Mount Vernon is the most popular historic home in the United States, visited by over a million people every year. A total of fourteen rooms are open to the public. Beautifully restored, they are painted in their original colors of green (a favorite color of Washington's) and vivid blues. The furniture, paintings, silver, porcelain, and rich window hangings are arranged as they were in George and Martha's time. Tours are available, led by volunteers in authentic period costumes who pause to chat about life at Mount Vernon when the Washingtons were alive.

You can also hear Mount Vernon's historic interpreters discuss the president, his life and his character, and explain how Washington set the standards of patriotism and honor that are still the benchmark for today's leaders.

Mount Vernon is located at the end of the Mount Vernon Highway, 8 miles south of Alexandria, Virginia, and 16 miles from downtown Washington, D.C. Open 365 days a year, April through August, 8 A.M. to 5 P.M.; March, September, and October, 9 A.M. to 5 P.M.; November through February, 9 A.M. to 4 P.M. Adults $8, senior citizens $7.50, children 6–11 $4.00, children 5 and under free. Group discounts. For more information: Mount Vernon Ladies Association, Mount Vernon, VA 22121. Telephone: 703-780-2000. Web site: http://www.mountvernon.org

John Adams

The distinguished family of President John Adams dominated the U.S. political scene as few have. His father was a member of his town board of selectmen. John held many government appointments, served as vice president under George Washington, and was chosen as the second president of the United States. He was also the father of a president (John Quincy Adams), the grandfather of a U.S. minister to Great Britain, and the great-grandfather of other illustrious politicians, writers, and historians.

He Sometimes Skipped Classes to Go Fishing

John Adams was born on October 30, 1735, in Braintree—now called Quincy—Massachusetts. As a boy, John liked to play marbles, fly kites, and sail toy boats. Although he was described as "chubby," he was an active child, roaming the woods and marshes, swimming and ice skating, fishing and hunting. Older boys taught him to smoke, a bad habit he continued for the rest of his life.

In John's family, in which children were encouraged to study and read for pleasure, John stood out like a sore thumb. He hated to read and disliked school. He was a poor student and sometimes skipped classes to go fishing.

By the time he was fourteen, John had finally accepted the fact that he must attend school. In fact, he found that he actually enjoyed it. In 1751, he was accepted at Harvard College. In addition to his regular studies, he joined a reading group and developed a gift for public speaking. It was also during this time that he started keeping the diary that has given us much important information about his life.

After graduating from Harvard, John began studying law with one of the finest attorneys in Massachusetts. John was an eloquent speaker, and he developed a consuming interest in politics and government. As time passed, he found that he especially enjoyed writing.

He sent manuscripts to several publications but had no luck getting them published. Finally, a series of humorous articles about New England farming, signed Humphrey Ploughjogger, was accepted by a Boston newspaper. Readers liked them so much that the articles ran all summer. He also began selling serious essays.

Adams, still a bachelor at twenty-eight, fell in love with nineteen-year-old Abigail Quincy Smith, the daughter of a minister in a nearby town. Nabby, as her friends called her, was a slender, soft-spoken girl with strong views on law, politics, and the rights of women. The marriage of these two independent people was an unusually happy one of "nearly perfect equality" that lasted for fifty-four years.

Nabby Smith

As a girl, Abigail Smith was one of the most popular young people in Boston. She was pretty and bright, and she loved to laugh and have fun. But best of all, she was kind and thoughtful. Her father taught her things most girls of that time did not learn. She was good at mathematics and was familiar with the politics of the thirteen colonies that later became the United States. And she was not afraid to speak her mind on most subjects, especially on education for women.

"The Most Insignificant Office"

In 1774 and 1775, Adams was chosen as a representative to the First and Second Continental Congresses in Philadelphia, where he helped other delegates draft the Declaration of Independence. During the Revolutionary War he served as commissioner to France, and in 1780, he was appointed as minister to the Netherlands. From 1785 to 1788 he was the first U.S. minister to England.

Following his return to the United States, he served under George Washington as the first vice president of the United States. Adams, an intelligent man with more than a touch of vanity, found it a frustrating job and complained to his wife, "My country in its wisdom has contrived for me the most insignificant office that ever the invention of man contrived or his imagination conceived."

Wandering in the Woods

When John Adams and his family were traveling to Washington, D.C., to move into the President's Mansion, they became lost in the woods north of the city. It was reported that they went in circles for several hours before finding the road that led to the capital.

The White House Had Just Been Built

As vice president, however, Adams became the natural choice for president when Washington declined a third term. He was elected in 1796 and served one term. The Adams family moved into the White House, then called the President's Mansion. The large East Room was still unfinished and Abigail Adams sometimes had the laundry hung there to dry. She felt it was undignified for the president's underwear to hang outside where people could see it flapping in the breeze.

Adams went on to create the Navy Department, the Marine Corps, and the Library of Congress (the national library, located in Washington, D.C.). During his term of office, the United States became a nation respected in international circles.

His life ended with a coincidence worthy of the movies. Both he and Thomas Jefferson, his close friend, died on July 4, 1826, the fiftieth anniversary of the signing of the Declaration of Independence. Adams was ninety years old when he died, the longest any president has lived so far.

☆ Visit the ADAMS National Historic Site ☆

The Adams National Historic Site, a 13-acre park in Quincy, Massachusetts, honors both John Adams and his son, John Quincy Adams, this country's sixth president. The adjacent houses on Franklin Street are the oldest presidential birthplaces in the nation. The two-story saltbox where John Adams was born dates back to about 1680. It has several fireplaces and low ceiling beams, and it is floored with wide planks.

Upon the death of his father, John Adams inherited the house next door, which became his home and law office, and the birthplace of his son, John Quincy. A door at the corner by the street was added for the use of John's clients. It was later boarded over but was found when the house was restored in 1896. The back door still has an old-fashioned latchstring that was put out to let in visitors.

The third house on the grounds was bought by John Adams when he was minister to England. It had been built as a country villa by a sugar planter from Jamaica. Abigail doubled the size of the place and the charming mansion became home to four generations of the Adams family.

Today, you can tour these historic houses and stroll the gravel paths through the orchard and formal gardens, where a white rosebush planted in 1788 still thrives today. Inside the "Old House," as it became known, you will see the china that Abigail Adams chose for the White House. The spectacles Adams wore lie on a beautiful tulipwood desk he bought in Europe, as if he had just laid them down for a moment.

Quincy is 8 miles south of Boston. The Adams National Historic Site is located at 1250 Hancock Street. Open daily April 19 to November 10, 9 A.M. to 5 P.M. Adults $2, children under 16 free. For more information: Adams National Historic Site, Visitor Center, 1250 Hancock Street, Quincy, MA 02269. Telephone: 617-770-1175. Web site: http://www.nps.gov/adam/

Thomas Jefferson

The third U.S. president, Thomas Jefferson, has been called our most gifted chief executive because of his many talents. He wrote the Declaration of Independence and was one of the creators of the Constitution. He was the first state governor to become president, the first president to have served as secretary of state, and the first president to found a university. Jefferson designed his own house and was an inventor, a scientist, and a violinist.

"Architecture Is My Delight"

Born on his family's Virginia plantation on April 13, 1743, Thomas was the third of ten children. He had a winning personality and a big smile, and he loved the outdoors. He would hike or ride the wild country for miles. But roaming the countryside wasn't all young Thomas did. He was expected to grow up to be a Virginia gentleman. For that, he had to study; he also learned to play the violin and dance the minuet and the Virginia reel.

When Thomas was fourteen years old, his father died, leaving his son many slaves and thousands of acres of land. Thomas became the head of the family, although an adult guardian stepped in until the boy was old enough to manage the plantation.

Thomas took to learning easily and did well in school and later at the College of William and Mary in Williamsburg, Virginia. He became interested in the law and served a five-year apprenticeship with a renowned attorney. Jefferson also was a member of the Virginia legislature.

The tall, red-haired young man with the high speaking voice began building a home on a small mountain on his property. He called it Monticello, which means "little mountain" in Italian.

Monticello was always a work in progress. Jefferson once said, "architecture is my delight, and putting up and pulling down one of my favorite amusements." From the day the foundation was laid until Jefferson's last breath, the house was built and rebuilt.

In 1770, Jefferson met Martha Wayles Skelton, a pretty widow of twenty-two with a baby son and a large estate. Jefferson began courting Martha, a charming woman who loved music as much as he did. She was also being courted by several other suitors.

A legend says that one evening two other gentlemen showed up on Martha's doorstep to visit. As they were being admitted into the house by the maid, they heard someone playing the violin, accompanied by a harpsichord, and a lady and a man singing. The men knew at once that it was Jefferson, for he was the only violinist in the neighborhood. They quickly excused themselves, and one said to the other, "We're wasting our time. We might as well go home."

Jefferson won Martha's heart and they were married in 1772. She had her own land and many slaves, left to her by her late husband. Although Jefferson called slavery "an abominable crime," he remained a slaveholder all his life. The question of slavery was one that would continue to haunt him.

British Soldiers Overran Monticello

In 1775, when he was only thirty-two years old, Jefferson traveled to Philadelphia as a member of the Second Continental Congress and helped to draft the Declaration of Independence. Then, during the Revolutionary War, Jefferson was governor of Virginia.

This was a sad time in his life, for in addition to the problems brought on by the war, British soldiers overran Monticello and two of Jefferson's other farms. But something far worse occurred. His thirty-three-year-old wife, Martha, died a few months after giving birth. This was but one in a series of tragedies the family experienced. Of the Jefferson children, only two, Martha, or Patsy as she was sometimes called, and her younger sister, Mary, called Polly, lived to adulthood. Three other daughters and a son died in infancy or early childhood. Martha's son by her first husband had also died, three years after she married Jefferson.

Following his wife's death, a heartbroken Jefferson moved to Paris to become the U.S. minister to France. When George Washington became president, he called Jefferson back from France to become secretary of state, but Jefferson left that post in 1793. He took a break from politics and withdrew to Monticello to remodel the house and concentrate on farming.

"A Splendid Misery"

By 1796, he was back in Washington as vice president under John Adams. Then, in the election of 1800, Jefferson defeated John Adams to become president, a post he called "a splendid misery" and one he would hold from 1801 to 1809.

The amiable Jefferson, who was sometimes plagued by migraine

Lewis and Clark

President Jefferson asked his former personal secretary, Meriwether Lewis, to follow the Mississippi River to its source to find an all-water route to the Pacific Ocean. Jefferson, an amateur naturalist, was also eager to learn the mysteries of what is now the northwestern part of the United States. Lewis chose William Clark, an older woodsman, soldier, and Indian fighter, as his second in command. The rest of the party consisted of Clark's black servant York, about thirty soldiers, and ten civilians.

They started off on May 14, 1804. After six months they were joined by a fur trapper and his Shoshone wife, Sacajawea, who helped the party communicate with the native inhabitants they encountered. The explorers went all the way to the Pacific Ocean and were gone approximately two years.

In their diaries, Lewis and Clark wrote about the geography and climate of the beautiful new land. They also brought back hundreds of plant and animal specimens.

headaches, enjoyed great popularity and became known as "the Man of the People" and "the Sage of Monticello." During his presidency he negotiated the Louisiana Purchase, acquiring vast new lands that stretched from the Atlantic to the Rockies and from the Gulf of Mexico to the Great Lakes and Canada. He also proposed the successful Lewis and Clark expedition to learn more about the lands in the Louisiana Purchase.

After his second term as president ended, Jefferson happily retired to Monticello. He liked to share the house with friends and constantly entertained hordes of visitors. People would come and stay for weeks. His two remaining children, Patsy and Polly, who had both married men from Virginia, were often at Monticello.

Finally, on July 4, 1826, exhausted, in poor health, and deeply in debt due to living beyond his means, Jefferson died. It was the fiftieth anniversary of the signing of the Declaration of Independence, the document he had written. His old friend, John Adams, the only other signer of the Declaration to become president, died the same day.

"Under the Influence of Flies"

During the signing of the Declaration of Independence, Congress met in a room near a horse stable that was full of flies. As the delegates argued, they constantly swatted flies with their handkerchiefs. Jefferson said that the flies finally got so bad that the members decided to sign the document just to get away from the torture. He often chuckled and said that the Declaration of Independence was signed "under the influence of flies."

☆ Visit ☆ MONTICELLO

Today, a guided tour leads you through the house and extensive grounds of Monticello to explore the many facets of Jefferson's life, including his love of architecture, gardening, farming, and science. Of special interest are some of his inventions: a two-faced clock that can be read outdoors as well as indoors, folding ladders, a dumbwaiter that carried dishes and food from the kitchen to the dining room, and an alcove bed that made it possible for Jefferson to rise in either his study or his bedroom.

Jefferson, a self-taught architect, designed the house to look like a building of ancient Rome. The three-story building has thirty-five rooms, plus twelve more in the basement, thirteen fireplaces, and eight stoves.

Since Jefferson didn't want to see the outbuildings from the house, he constructed long terraces to hide them. He connected the two terraces with an underground passage.

Monticello is 3 miles south of Charlottesville, Virginia. Open daily, except Christmas, March through October, 8 A.M. to 5 P.M.; November through February, 9 A.M. to 4:30 P.M. Adults $9, children 6–11 $5. Student discounts. For more information: Monticello, Box 316, Charlottesville, VA 22902. Telephone: 804-984-9800. Web site: http://www.monticello.org

James Madison

James Madison, the fourth president of the United States, served from 1809 to 1817. He was a shy man with a quiet speaking voice who played the leading role in creating the Constitution. He stood 5 feet 4 inches tall, weighed barely 100 pounds, and had bright blue eyes under bushy eyebrows. He always dressed in black and was the first president to wear trousers instead of knee breeches. At Madison's inauguration, some said he looked like a little old man standing beside his wife, the beautiful Dolley.

He Studied Such Long Hours That He Nearly Ruined His Health

James was born on March 16, 1751, in Port Conway, Virginia. He was the firstborn of twelve children. James was sent away at an early age to study at another plantation. This was fine with the little boy, who loved to read and enjoyed studying. He was not lonely away from home, either, for five of his cousins were studying with him. Later he was tutored at home with his siblings.

When he was eighteen years old, James traveled ten to twelve days to New Jersey to attend the College of New Jersey (now called Princeton University). It was a hard and sometimes dangerous journey, crossing rain-swollen rivers and rough mountain passes, but he enjoyed seeing the new country.

James was happy at Princeton, but he studied such long hours that he nearly ruined his health. He hoped to graduate in two years, so he carried a double load, which was almost too much for him. He also stayed up late night after night, discussing with other students a revolution against England and independence for the colonies.

After finishing his university courses, he returned home to tutor his younger brothers and sisters. This proved to be a depressing task. The children were not interested in studying and wouldn't do anything he asked.

"The Work of Many Heads"

James had become interested in politics at Princeton, and now he became politically active in Virginia. In 1780, he served as a Virginia delegate to the Second Continental Congress in Philadelphia to approve the Constitution.

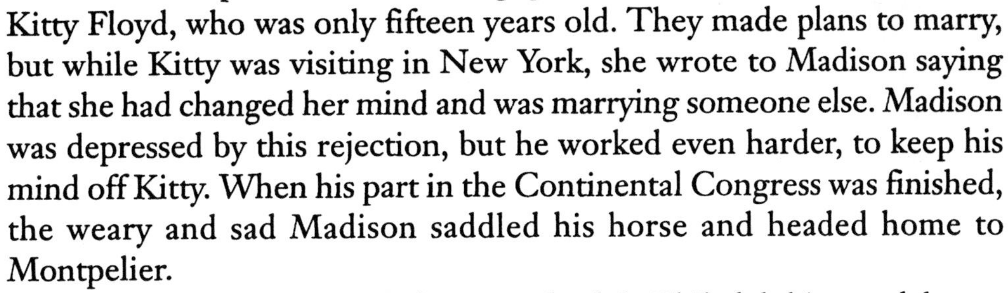

While the thirty-two year-old Madison was in Philadelphia, he became engaged to Kitty Floyd, who was only fifteen years old. They made plans to marry, but while Kitty was visiting in New York, she wrote to Madison saying that she had changed her mind and was marrying someone else. Madison was depressed by this rejection, but he worked even harder, to keep his mind off Kitty. When his part in the Continental Congress was finished, the weary and sad Madison saddled his horse and headed home to Montpelier.

But by May 25, 1787, Madison was back in Philadelphia as a delegate to the Constitutional Convention. By September of the same year the delegates signed the Constitution. In later years Madison was called the "Father of the Constitution" because of his tireless work in getting it adopted. This bothered Madison, who said that the document was not "the offspring of a single brain, but the work of many heads and hands."

Madison was forty-three when he met the vivacious, blue-eyed Dolley Payne Todd, a twenty-five-year-old widow with one child. She had slipped on a patch of icy pavement. The bachelor reached out a hand to steady her and was rewarded with one of her gorgeous smiles.

Madison was instantly attracted and waged a whirlwind courtship. Although Dolley didn't fall for Madison right away, she accepted his proposal of marriage, hoping the respect and admiration that she felt for him would turn into love, as it did. She became one of the most popular women who ever lived in the White House.

Dolley Grabbed Her Caged Parrot and Headed for Virginia

Madison served as Thomas Jefferson's secretary of state. When Jefferson retired after two terms, Madison easily won the election and was inaugurated as president on March 4, 1809.

The United States was at that time on the brink of war with England over freedom of the seas. During this War of 1812, British troops staged a surprise raid on Washington, looting and burning public buildings. President Madison was out of town inspecting a battlefield, but Dolley was in the President's Mansion planning a dinner party for forty guests.

Madison sent word to Dolley that the British were on their way to the mansion and urged her to leave immediately. Cool and unflappable, Dolley swiftly cut a portrait of George Washington out of its frame and packed it with her things, grabbed her caged parrot, and headed for Virginia to meet her husband.

The President's Mansion was burned, but thanks to Dolley's coolness in a crisis, a priceless historical artifact was saved—and so was her parrot!

"Our Hearts Understand Each Other"

Dolley decorated the president's quarters in bright yellow and was the first hostess to serve that new treat, ice cream, in the great mansion. She was friendly to everyone, and people said that her "gracious tact smoothed over many a quarrel." The Madisons were one of Washington's most devoted couples. Dolley often said about herself and Madison, "our hearts understand each other."

Madison's last two years as president were triumphant. At the end of his second term, he and Dolley were cheered by huge crowds as they left Washington to return to their beloved Montpelier. Although they made the plantation their permanent home, the Madisons didn't retire from public life. The pair were still involved in national and world affairs. Madison kept up a voluminous correspondence and Dolley entertained just as lavishly at Montpelier as she had at the White House.

☆ Visit ☆ MONTPELIER

Montpelier was opened to the public in March 1987 as part of the bicentennial celebration of the U.S. Constitution. Rolling pasturelands, formal gardens, and old-growth forest surround the home of James Madison. Few of the Madison furnishings remain, since Dolley sold most of them when she moved back to Washington after James's death. You'll learn about the history of Montpelier from the "acoustiguide audio tour" and see Dolley Madison's silver snuff box and the engagement ring given to her by James. The tour does not cover the entire house, but there are exhibits on the main floor and tours of the outside area.

The James Madison Museum is a few miles away in Orange, Virginia. Exhibits there trace the life and times of the fourth president and his First Lady. Displays include some of Dolley's clothes and the Madisons' correspondence and books.

Montpelier is 4 miles south of Orange, Virginia. Open daily, except New Year's Day, the first Saturday in November, Thanksgiving, Christmas Eve, Christmas, and New Year's Eve, April through November, 9:30 A.M. to 4:30 P.M.; December through March, 9:30 A.M. to 3:00 P.M. Adults $7.50, children 6–11 $3.50. For more information: Montpelier, 11407 Constitution Highway, Montpelier Station, VA 22957. Telephone: 540-672-2728. Web site: http://www.montpelier.org

James Monroe

James Monroe was one of four Virginians who governed the United States during the first thirty-six years of the republic's existence. His two terms as chief executive have been called "the era of good feeling." There were no wars, and the country was rapidly expanding. The greatest milestone of his administration, however, was a speech he gave that came to be known as the Monroe Doctrine. The Monroe Doctrine declared that the United States would not tolerate European interference in the Americas and promised that it would not intrude on other governments or established colonies.

He Took the Most Difficult Courses

Born on his father's large tobacco farm in Westmoreland County, Virginia, on April 28, 1758, James was the oldest of five children. Little is known of his boyhood since he rarely wrote or spoke about his early years once he was an adult.

When he was sixteen years old, James enrolled at the College of William and Mary in Williamsburg, Virginia, where he took the most difficult courses offered: advanced mathematics, chemistry, biology, astronomy, physics, literature, and law. We know that he also signed a student petition complaining about the terrible dormitory food!

James Felt His Place Was Fighting for His Country

When word came that his family's friend George Washington was now commander in chief of the Continental Army, James felt his place was fighting for his country instead of attending school.

When he was eighteen, the tall, muscular youth joined the Third Virginia Regiment as a lieutenant. During one difficult battle, Monroe became a hero when he led his battalion in a wild charge after his captain had been hurt. A bullet ripped through Monroe's shoulder, and he was carried from the battlefield. In 1780, he was appointed lieutenant colonel at only twenty-three years of age.

More Public Offices Than Any Other President

After the war, Monroe studied law with Thomas Jefferson, who was then the governor of Virginia. Before he could open a law office, a group of citizens asked him to run for the Virginia legislature. He was elected without opposition. Busy as he was, he still found time to enjoy himself by going to horse races and playing cards with friends.

In June 1783, he was elected to the Confederation Congress, the first meeting of the national government after the war. The 1785–1786 session of Congress met in New York City. While there, the twenty-seven-year-old Monroe, who had long told friends that he would never marry, changed his mind about matrimony.

He and Elizabeth Kortright, a dark-eyed beauty of seventeen from a prominent family, fell madly in love. Monroe waged a brief but intense courtship. Within weeks they were married. The young couple lived with her father until the congressional meetings were over and then returned to Virginia, where Monroe opened a law office.

In 1793, James and Elizabeth bought land in Charlottesville, Virginia, to be near their good friend Thomas Jefferson at Monticello. Although Monroe's 600-acre plantation, Highland, was not as elaborate as Monticello, it was far from simple, with elegant furnishings that you can see today. The Monroes' first guests were James and Dolley Madison.

Monroe held more public offices than any other president. He was appointed minister to France in 1794. Following that, he served as governor of Virginia. From 1814 to 1815, Monroe was James Madison's secretary of state and also briefly replaced the secretary of war.

The Trip Was a Tremendous Success

James Monroe was elected president in 1816 and served until 1825. He was unable to move his family into the White House after he was elected because it had not been rebuilt after the fire in 1814. The Monroes lived in rented houses, and he also toured the United States until the White House was ready for occupancy. He wanted to see the country he would be governing. He was gone for fifteen weeks and the trip was a tremendous success. Everywhere he went, people crowded the roadsides to get a glimpse of their president and cheered him.

The Monroes finally moved into the White House in 1817 with their younger daughter, Maria. (Their older daughter, Eliza, was already married and living away from home.) Elizabeth decorated it with French furniture and silverware that had belonged to Queen Marie Antoinette.

When everything was in place, the elegant Elizabeth, who was one of our most fashionable First Ladies, gave a gala reception for the diplomatic corps to show off the renovated White House. Although most guests were approving, some, who were used to Dolley Madison's thoroughly American ways, felt that Mrs. Monroe was snooty because of her more formal manner.

On the other hand, Monroe prided himself on being down-to-earth. He had little interest in fashionable clothes and at a time when most men were wearing trousers, Monroe still clung to knee breeches and buckled shoes. He wore his hair in a pigtail, though shorter hair was the style. Monroe also wore an out-of-style hat with a cockade (a feather ornament), which most men had long ago discarded.

In the last years of his life, Monroe was so heavily in debt that he was forced to sell Highland. He spent a great deal of time trying to collect money he said the government owed him for expenses incurred during his long years of public service. Congress finally awarded him $30,000, which was enough to pay off his creditors. Monroe died on July 4, 1831, in New York City, at the age of eighty-five. He was the third president to die on the anniversary of the country's independence.

Unusual White House Guests

While Monroe was president, six Native American chiefs came to visit, bringing three women and a small child. They talked to the president in French, English, and several Indian languages. The visiting tribespeople wore only breech cloths, body paint, and beads. When they returned a few days later, someone had dressed them in store-bought clothes and the men were wearing three-piece suits!

☆ Visit ☆ Ash Lawn-Highland

Today, Monroe's alma mater, the College of William and Mary, owns and administers Ash Lawn-Highland. ("Ash Lawn" was the name given to the plantation after it was sold by Monroe.) French wallpapers, priceless period furniture, fine paintings, and other art objects fill the rooms. The house is also a museum dedicated to Monroe's achievements, with the entrance showcasing the documents of the Monroe Doctrine.

Large peacocks strut the spacious lawns just as they did when the Monroes lived there. The still-working farm features craft demonstrations of candle and Christmas ornament making, tinsmithing, and open-hearth cooking. There's even a Dairy Products Workshop where participants can churn butter.

James Monroe would be pleased that Ash Lawn-Highland generates enough income each year to provide $50,000 for James Monroe Merit Scholarships for outstanding William and Mary students.

Ash Lawn-Highland is 2.5 miles south of Monticello on Virginia State Route 795. Open daily, except New Year's Day, Thanksgiving, and Christmas, March through October, 9 A.M. to 6 P.M.; November through February, 10 A.M. to 5 P.M. Adults $7. Student discounts. For more information: Ash Lawn-Highland, Route 6 Box 37, Charlottesville, VA 22902-8722. Telephone: 804-293-9539. Web site: http://www.avenue.org/ashlawn

John Quincy Adams

John Quincy Adams was the only president whose father was also a president. He served from 1825 to 1829 and after his term of office, he was elected to Congress by his district in Massachusetts. He was a powerful congressman who championed the cause of civil rights and fought slavery.

A Child of the Revolution

Our sixth president was born in Braintree (now Quincy), Massachusetts, on July 11, 1767. He was the second child and the oldest of three sons of Abigail and John Adams. John Quincy's mother was sure he would become president of the United States and never let him forget that the weight of the highest office in the land would rest on his shoulders some day.

John Quincy was truly a child of the Revolution. From the time of his birth, the colonists had been rebelling against British rule. One day John Quincy's older cousin took the two-year-old boy to see the "redcoats," British troops who were stationed near the Adamses' house. The tiny child never forgot the sight of those troops in their scarlet greatcoats parading to the rattle of drums, their guns and bayonets glinting in the sun.

Six years later, with spyglass in hand, eight-year-old John Quincy scrambled up a rocky ledge near his house to watch the Battle of Bunker Hill, the first real fighting of the Revolutionary War.

In 1778, his father, John Adams, was sent to France to bring that country into the war on the side of the thirteen colonies. John Quincy, only eleven years old, accompanied him on a ship named the *Boston*. The unlucky *Boston* was chased by British warships, plowed through a violent storm, and ran into a pirate ship, which the *Boston* crew fought and captured.

Through it all, John Quincy remained calm and courageous. The sailors taught him the names of the various sails and how and when they were used. They also instructed him in tying nautical knots. He even learned French from some fellow passengers.

He lived with his father in Europe, spending time in the Netherlands, Russia, Sweden, Denmark, and Germany as well as France. It was an exciting life, traveling and meeting world leaders. During this time he began writing in a diary every day, a habit he continued for the rest of his life. (His journals eventually filled twelve volumes!)

What He Really Enjoyed Was Writing

At the age of eighteen, John Quincy returned home to enter Harvard. He graduated in 1787 and moved to Newburyport, Massachusetts, to study with an attorney. What he really enjoyed, however, was writing.

By 1790, he was practicing law in Boston and writing political essays on the side. Some of John Quincy's pieces were read by President George Washington. In 1794, Washington appointed the twenty-seven-year-old writer-attorney as ambassador to the Netherlands.

While on a diplomatic mission to London, John Quincy began courting Louisa Johnson, the oldest daughter of the U.S. consul to England, Joshua Johnson, and his English wife. He soon asked her to marry him. When his parents heard that he was engaged to an English girl (even though she had an American father), they tried to break up the romance, but to no avail. The pair were married and moved to Berlin. John Quincy was appointed ambassador to Prussia by his father, John Adams, who had become president of the United States.

After four years in Berlin, the couple returned to the United States. John Quincy resumed his law practice, but he was dissatisfied and bored. Louisa, who was used to city life, also had a hard time adjusting to the "Yankee farm community" of Braintree.

John Quincy was itching to get back into politics. In 1802, he was elected to the state senate and in 1803 he served in the U.S. Senate. Six years later, he was appointed ambassador to Russia. He and Louisa placed their two older sons in boarding school and left for Russia with their two-year-old son. Following that assignment, John Quincy held the same post in England. He was steadily climbing the political ladder. His next stop before the presidency was as secretary of state under James Madison.

"That Dull and Stately Prison"

The second President Adams was inaugurated on March 4, 1825, after defeating Andrew Jackson, William Crawford, and Henry Clay. Most of his progressive ideas, such as connecting the country with a network of highways, establishing a department of interior to conserve natural resources, and funding the creative arts, were shot down by the public. Americans would have none of these public works except the Erie Canal, which was already finished. They said his plans would give the federal government too much power.

Legend says that while John Quincy was in the White House, he rose every morning at five o'clock, built a fire, read his Bible, and then went swimming in the Potomac River before anyone else was awake. Supposedly, one morning as he was taking his daily plunge, Anne Royall, a writer and reporter, crept up the bank and trapped the president by sitting on his clothes until he gave her an interview.

The Adventures of a Nobody

Louisa Adams resented the position of women in her world and wrote that in the future "timid women" would not allow men to treat them as inferiors. She was so miserable much of the time she was in the White House that she titled one of her manuscripts *The Adventures of a Nobody*. Today, hundreds of pages in Louisa's handwriting lie in libraries among the Adams family papers.

We know more about Louisa Adams than we do about many early presidents' wives because she kept a record of her time in Washington, D.C. She hated living at the White House and spent many lonely hours "scribbling, scribbling, scribbling." She called the mansion "that dull and stately prison in which the sounds of mirth are seldom heard."

Although John Quincy may not have been a very successful president, he got a second chance to use his leadership skills as a member of the House of Representatives, where he served until two days before his death.

☆ Visit the ☆ ADAMS National Historic Site

The thirteen-acre Adams National Historic Site is shared by the second and sixth presidents of the United States—John Adams and his son, John Quincy Adams. For more information on the Adams National Historic Site, see page 10.

Andrew Jackson

For over forty years, wealthy gentlemen from Virginia and members of the Adams family of Massachusetts had monopolized the presidency. Now that the United States was no longer just a small group of states along the Atlantic seacoast, but a big sprawling country, a new kind of man was needed to fill the job of president. Andrew Jackson, a two-fisted western frontiersman, was that man.

Andrew Was a Rebel

Andrew Jackson came from a poor South Carolina family. His father died a few days before he was born on March 15, 1767. The third of three sons, Andrew had little direction, was undisciplined, and was always in trouble because of his hot temper.

Andrew attended enough classes in the local Presbyterian church to learn to read and write, skills most children and even adults of that time did not have. To the end of his life, however, he never mastered grammar and was always a poor speller, but he was an eloquent and fiery speaker.

At the age of thirteen, Andrew ran away to become a courier in the Revolutionary War. He was captured by British forces and held prisoner, but even behind enemy lines, Andrew was a rebel. When ordered to polish a British officer's boots, the boy refused and was rewarded with a whack on the head from a sword. Throughout his life Jackson carried the scar proudly as a symbol of his defiance.

Hot-Tempered and Fearless

For all his rough ways and troublemaking, the blue-eyed young Jackson had a strong sense of his own abilities and was determined to make something of himself. He studied law and settled in Tennessee, where he became a successful district attorney. He went on to serve as Tennessee's first representative in the U.S. Congress.

During the time Jackson was practicing law, he lived in a boardinghouse in Nashville that was run by a widow with an unhappily married daughter named Rachel. The dark-haired young woman had left her husband after a violent quarrel and came to live with her mother. Jackson was attracted to Rachel, but he did not pursue her because she was a married woman.

In time, Rachel received word that her husband had divorced her. When Jackson heard this news, he proposed to her, and they were soon married. Two years later, the couple found that their marriage was not legal because there had never been an official divorce.

Rachel and Andrew quickly remarried as soon as her divorce was final. Still, Jackson's enemies gossiped and started many unkind rumors about Rachel's divorce. Deeply in love with his wife and never one to ignore an insult, Jackson defended her honor more than once. The marriage lasted seventeen years, and they were devoted to each other until her death just before he became president.

Throughout most of his life, Jackson was hot-tempered and fearless, two characteristics that sometimes landed him in trouble. Until he mellowed in later years, it took very little to provoke a fight with Jackson. He fought in several duels, but only one was fatal.

This particular affair of honor took place over a disagreement about a horse race. Charles Dickinson, a notorious slave trader, called Jackson "a worthless scoundrel," "a coward," and he also insulted Jackson's wife.

These slurs were too much for Jackson, who challenged the name-caller to a duel even though he knew Dickinson was a nearly perfect shot.

The two met on a hill on May 30, 1806. They stalked 24 feet apart, pistols pointed to the ground. Dickinson fired the first shot. The bullet slammed Jackson in the chest. He reeled back from the impact. Then with the coolness that would make him a hero in battle, he clamped one hand over the wound to control the bleeding and slowly took aim. The terrified slave trader had the choice of standing his ground or running and being called a coward for the rest of his life. Dickinson chose to stand. Jackson's bullet struck him below the ribs and he died a few minutes later.

The Spokesman for the Ordinary People

Jackson became a national hero in the War of 1812. He returned home from battle as the general of the U.S. forces who had defeated the British in the Battle of New Orleans. During this time he earned the nickname "Old Hickory" because his troops boasted, "He's as tough as hickory."

Jackson was nominated for president in 1828 and won the election. Many Americans considered him to be the spokesman for the ordinary people. At his inauguration, the thousands of frontiersmen, working men, and farmers who had voted for him descended upon Washington, D.C., to show their support. They clambered on rooftops, crowded sidewalks, and blocked traffic to get a glimpse of him.

Following the ceremony, Jackson invited everybody to the White House for refreshments. And he really meant everybody! Wearing their leather breeches, sheepskin coats, muddy boots, and coonskin caps, they packed the place. In their eagerness to miss nothing, they knocked over punch bowls and tables. Fistfights started and women fainted. People climbed on the velvet-covered chairs to cheer the new president. Unfortunately, a lot of the food was trampled into the carpet along with chicken bones, tobacco juice, and whiskey. Waiters finally had to move the food tables onto the White House lawn to save the place from being completely wrecked!

Nevertheless, Jackson continued holding mass receptions and inviting ordinary citizens to dinner throughout his administration. At his last reception, a group of Jackson's admirers lugged in a huge wheel of cheddar cheese as a present for their hero. According to witnesses, the smell of cheese lingered in the White House for weeks.

Assassination Attempt

Andrew Jackson was the first president to survive an assassination attempt. Richard Lawrence, a mentally unbalanced housepainter, tried to kill him at the funeral of one of Jackson's friends. Lawrence fired two pistols at the president from only 6 feet away, but both guns misfired. The fearless Jackson chased after Lawrence, caught him, and began beating him with his cane. Lawrence had sorely underestimated his target! The man was later judged insane and committed to a mental institution for the rest of his life.

"The Old Spoiler"

Despite his quick temper and acid tongue, Jackson was essentially kind and tender, especially toward women and children. He and Rachel loved children, but they had none of their own, although they adopted Rachel's nephew, who became their heir.

Andrew and Rachel delighted in every moment they spent at their plantation, the Hermitage. Visitors, knowing Jackson's sometimes rough ways, were often surprised at the elegance of the house. The interior was comfortably furnished with French beds, the finest table silver and crystal, and hand-painted wallpapers. At the Hermitage, the man the nation knew as "Old Hickory" became the loving person his family called "the Old Spoiler."

After dodging bullets, swords, arrows, and tomahawks, Jackson died in his own bed at the Hermitage at the age of seventy-eight, surrounded by the members of his household.

☆ Visit the ☆ HERMITAGE

In 1974 the Hermitage, a Greek revival–style mansion, was fully restored by the Ladies Hermitage Association and is now a museum devoted to Jackson's life and achievements. It is the fourth most visited presidential home in the United States after the White House, Mount Vernon, and Monticello.

You approach the house by a driveway bordered by large evergreen trees that Jackson planted in 1838. One of the most eye-catching decorating details in the mansion is the wallpaper in the front hall, which depicts the Greek hero Telemachus in search of his father, Odysseus, on the island of Calypso.

The Hermitage stages several summer workshops for children. You can participate in an archaeological dig or learn about slave life by washing clothes on a scrub board, ironing and folding napkins, stringing beans, churning butter, kneading dough, and doing other chores on the working farm.

The Hermitage is located just off Old Hickory Boulevard in Nashville, Tennessee. Open daily, except the third week of January, Thanksgiving, and Christmas, 9 A.M. to 5 P.M. Adults $9.50. Student discounts. For more information: The Hermitage, 4580 Rachel's Lane, Hermitage, TN 37076. Telephone: 615-889-2941. Web site: http://www. thehermitage.com

Martin Van Buren

Martin Van Buren was the first president born after the signing of the Declaration of Independence and the first president born a U.S. citizen. He was never a popular leader like Andrew Jackson, but Van Buren stood up for his convictions. For instance, he hated slavery and did his best to abolish the practice.

He Grew Up Speaking Dutch

Born on December 5, 1782, in the Hudson River Valley village of Kinderhook, New York, the eighth president of the United States was of Dutch descent and grew up speaking Dutch at home. Almost everyone in town came from Holland, and most of them were related. Martin had four brothers and sisters and three step-siblings. Their father kept a tavern that became a meeting place for political groups and local officials.

Martin often helped his father in the tavern after school, sweeping floors, carrying firewood, and doing other chores. There he sometimes saw such famous politicians as Alexander Hamilton and Aaron Burr. Martin enjoyed hearing these men talk of issues that were important to the country, and he soon developed an interest in politics.

By the time he was fifteen years old, Martin was studying law. He worked hard, and by 1806, Van Buren was considered one of the best lawyers in the state, even though he was only twenty-four years old. In 1807 he was appointed as counselor to the state supreme court. He married his childhood sweetheart, Hannah Hoes, a distant cousin on his mother's side. Hannah was small and slim like her husband, and people commented on how well they looked together. The young couple set up housekeeping in a little frame house in Kinderhook, but within a year they moved to the town of Hudson.

"The Little Magician"

In 1821 Van Buren was elected to the U.S. Senate. He was known for his crafty style of politics. He was good-tempered and always ready with a smile, a handshake, and a joke. In fact, Van Buren became so good at reaching his political goals that people called him "the Little Magician." Eleven days after leaving the Senate in 1829, he became the governor of New York State. He resigned that post after only sixty-four days to serve as Andrew Jackson's secretary of state. Then in 1833, he became Jackson's vice president.

Van Buren was elected president in 1836 and moved into the White House with his four bachelor sons. The great house lacked a First Lady, since Hannah had died some years earlier and Van Buren had not remarried. (He was the third president to live in the White House as a widower.) Dolley Madison, the former president's wife, set about finding a wife for the president's oldest son, for she felt the White House needed a woman's touch. Dolley was a successful matchmaker and Andrew Van Buren married the beautiful Angelica Singleton. The happy pair made their home in the White House and Angelica became her father-in-law's hostess at state affairs.

During Van Buren's administration the country was caught up in a depression and the people blamed the president. As a result he became wildly unpopular. During these hard times, Van Buren wore a coat with a velvet

Scenic Washington, D.C.

During Van Buren's time, Washington, D.C., had a population of about 40,000. The area was swampy and full of malaria-carrying mosquitoes. Pigs rooted for garbage along the streets. It is said that Charles Dickens, visiting from London, took one look at the city and was horrified, especially by the open sewers that ran down the broad avenues.

collar and tight gloves made of the softest leather. He rode in a grand carriage, attended by footmen in uniform. Van Buren's political rivals used this love of luxury against him when he ran for a second term. As a result, in 1840 he was soundly defeated by William Henry Harrison.

The day after Harrison's inauguration, Van Buren set out for Lindenwald (Dutch for "grove of linden trees"), the estate he had bought while he was still president. Just 2 miles outside Kinderhook, the beautiful two-story brick mansion was situated on more than 220 acres, including formal gardens, ornamental fishponds, wooded paths, and farmland. Van Buren lived a happy and busy life there, traveling and taking an active role in politics until he died on July 24, 1862.

☆ Visit ☆ LINDENWALD

Today, Lindenwald is a 22-acre National Historic Site and a unit of the National Park Service. The house has been restored to what it was like when Van Buren lived there. With imported French wallpapers, Brussels carpets, silk draperies, oil paintings, and fine furniture, it is the house of a man who enjoyed living in elegance.

Ranger-led walks and bicycle tours are conducted through approximately 3 miles of wooded trails of the Martin Van Buren Natural Area. Throughout the year many special events are available to visitors. In the fall, there are nature walks through the fall foliage. Nordic skiing, snowshoeing, and other activities take place over designated trails in the winter. On December 5, Van Buren's birthday is celebrated with a cake, speeches, special programs, and singing. Lindenwald is still a happy place. No wonder the former president said that he "drank the pure pleasure of life" when he was there.

The Martin Van Buren National Historic Site is in Kinderhook, New York, 18 miles south of Albany. Open daily mid-May through October, and weekends in November through the first week in December, 9 A.M. to 4:30 P.M. (Schedule subject to change.) Adults $2, children under 17 free. For more information: Superintendent, Martin Van Buren National Historic Site, 1013 Old Post Road, Kinderhook, NY 12106. Telephone: 518-758-9689. Web site: http://www.nps.gov/mava

William Henry Harrison

William Henry Harrison's term as president was shockingly brief. He died of pneumonia only a month after his inauguration, becoming the first chief executive to die while in office. As a result, he left little legacy other than his earlier heroism and military leadership on the American frontier. Harrison is the only president whose grandson, Benjamin Harrison, was also president.

At Twelve, He Set a Horse's Broken Leg

William Henry Harrison, the youngest of seven children of a wealthy Virginia farmer, Benjamin Harrison, was born on February 9, 1773. Benjamin served in that state's legislature and later became its governor. He was also one of the signers of the Declaration of Independence.

When William Henry was a small boy, a unit of German soldiers fighting for the British Army during the Revolution set fire to Richmond, Virginia. The troops moved on to Berkeley Plantation, the Harrisons' estate, but the family had enough advance warning to escape.

The Harrison children were schooled at home by private tutors. William Henry was not a good student, however, and his parents were usually disappointed in his grades. But from an early age, the little boy was interested in medicine, always bandaging somebody's wound or attempting to treat them when they were ill. At twelve, he set a horse's broken leg. The veterinarian, arriving late, congratulated him on the good job he had done and left.

At the age of fourteen, the thin-faced youth began pre-medical studies. William Henry later studied medicine in Philadelphia but quit after two years—against his family's wishes—to join the army fighting Indians on America's frontier.

"A Lowly Indian Fighter"

Harrison received an officer's commission from George Washington and was given command of eighty new recruits.

In 1795, Harrison took three weeks' leave from the army and went to visit friends in Kentucky. There he met Anna Symmes, the well-educated daughter of a prosperous judge. The young couple fell in love, but when Harrison asked for Anna's hand in marriage, the judge forbade her to see her suitor again, saying that she deserved better than "a lowly Indian fighter." William Henry convinced Anna to elope with him and share his life in the wild Northwest Territory, an area between the Ohio and the Mississippi Rivers. The couple had ten children, and only the youngest, James, failed to survive to adulthood. The Harrison family was unusually healthy for that time, when many families lost as many as half their children to childhood diseases.

In 1800, the great tract of land known as the Northwest Territory was broken into two parts, the Ohio and Indiana Territories, and the twenty-seven-year-old Harrison was appointed governor of the Indiana Territory. Harrison, who was also secretary of Indian affairs for the territory, negotiated with the Shawnee Indians to open large areas of land for settlement by the white man. But when hordes of settlers overran their hunting ground, the Shawnees rebelled. Harrison and Chief Tecumseh were unable to work out the land dispute, and both sides geared up for battle.

In 1811, Tecumseh led his warriors in a surprise attack on Governor Harrison and his troops, who were camped at the junction of Tippecanoe Creek and the Wabash River. The Shawnees killed and wounded a large number of the soldiers, but Harrison rallied. He drove the warriors back and destroyed the village of Tecumseh's brother.

The Battle of Tippecanoe made Harrison famous and earned him the nickname of "Old Tippecanoe," which became the rallying cry of his election campaign in 1840.

He Led a Parade to the White House in Freezing Weather

Harrison defeated Martin Van Buren to become the ninth president of the United States. At his inauguration in March 1841, he stood out in a cold wind without coat, hat, or gloves and gave the longest inauguration speech in U.S. history. He spoke for almost two hours! Following the speech, he led a parade to the White House in freezing weather. That night, after such an exhausting day, he attended three formal balls. The next morning he woke with a severe cold and by April 3, he was dead of pneumonia.

Following his death, his wife, Anna, received the sum of $25,000, the first pension to be given a president's widow. Anna had been too ill to attend her husband's inauguration. She had just begun packing her household goods for the trip to Washington, D.C., when she received word that Harrison was dead.

TECUMSEH

Tecumseh's name means "Shooting Star" in the Shawnee language. Legend says that Tecumseh started hating white people when he was just a child because a group of white men killed his father. His hatred grew when white soldiers burned his village, forcing Tecumseh, his sisters, and his brothers to hide in the woods for days. Later, Tecumseh said that he could not look at a white man's face without feeling his flesh crawl.

In the battle for the territory in Indiana, the young Shawnee chief would become General William Henry Harrison's most bitter enemy. During the War of 1812, Harrison, a brigadier general, once more faced Tecumseh. Out to get revenge, the tribal leader had joined the British against the Americans. At the Battle of the Thames, Tecumseh was finally killed.

☆ Visit ☆ BERKELEY PLANTATION

Today, President Harrison's birthplace and boyhood home, Berkeley Plantation, is open to the public. This historic site was acquired by the Harrison family in 1691.

During the Civil War, General Daniel Butterfield composed the melody "Taps" while staying at Berkeley Plantation. The tune was quickly taken up by both the Union and Confederate armies. "Taps" is the bugle call signaling the end of the day in the military. It is also played at funerals of those who have served in the military.

The handsome Georgian mansion at Berkeley is the oldest three-story brick house in Virginia. All the rooms are furnished with fine antiques and furniture of the period. The house is surrounded by 1,400 acres, which include gardens, beautiful boxwood hedges, and acres of manicured lawns that slope to the flowing James River. After his election, Harrison returned to the bedroom where he was born to write his inaugural address at a small desk that is still there.

Berkeley Plantation is halfway between Richmond and Williamsburg, at 12602 Harrison Landing Road in Charles City, Virginia. The mansion and grounds are open daily, except Christmas, 9 A.M. to 5 P.M. Adults $8. Student discounts. For more information: Berkeley Plantation, 12602 Harrison Landing Road, Charles City, VA 23030. Telephone: 804-829-6018. Web site: http://www.berkeleyplantation.com

John Tyler

John Tyler, who served from 1841 to 1845, has been called the "accidental" president. He was the first vice president to succeed a president who died in office. Everyone thought Tyler would simply act as caretaker when William Henry Harrison died a month after taking office. Instead he assumed all the duties of the office of president. In doing so, he set a precedent for later vice presidents in the same circumstances.

John Learned to Love Music

John, one of eight children, was born on March 29, 1790. His father was a well-to-do judge who had gone to law school with Thomas Jefferson. The Tyler family lived in luxury on a 1,220-acre plantation with at least forty slaves. When the little boy was seven years old, his mother died, and his father doubled his attentions to the children. Evenings, they would sit on the lawn while Judge Tyler played his violin or told stories. It was here that John learned to love music and began to play the fiddle himself.

Although John was kind and got along well with people, he could be tough. When he was ten, he led his schoolmates in a rebellion against a teacher who was cruel to them. Unable to stand the tyrant another moment, the boys grabbed Mr. McMurdo, threw him down, and tied him up. They locked the schoolroom and left the struggling teacher behind his desk. It was late afternoon before he was rescued. When the irate schoolmaster complained to John's father, Tyler sent the teacher packing, saying that there was no place for tyranny in the schoolroom.

"I Can Never Consent to Being Dictated To"

After finishing college, John apprenticed with his father. At twenty-one, John was a practicing attorney with a brilliant courtroom manner and his father was governor of Virginia. Two years later, John was elected to the Virginia House of Delegates. Since his career was going well, Tyler could now propose to Letitia Christian, a girl from a nearby plantation. She was lovely but shy, and John later said that he did not dare to kiss her hand until three weeks before the wedding! They were married on the bridegroom's birthday and lived happily together, although Letitia rarely appeared with John in public. She seemed happy to stay at home with their eight children.

Tyler's career progressed nicely. After serving five terms in the Virginia legislature, Tyler was elected to the U.S. House of Representatives in 1817. He became the governor of Virginia and then served in the U.S. Senate. In 1840 he became vice president under William Henry Harrison.

When Tyler took over the presidency following Harrison's death, his cabinet told him that they considered him an "acting" president who was expected to do as he was told. Tyler politely informed the men that "I shall be pleased to avail myself of your counsel and advice. But I can never consent to being dictated to as to what I shall and shall not do. When you think otherwise your resignation will be accepted."

Tyler ended the war with the Seminole Indians by simply declaring that the war was over. He promised the handful of Seminoles who had hidden in the swamps of Florida that they would no longer be pursued by U.S. forces. Tyler, who was an advocate of slavery, annexed Texas as a slave state just before he left office in 1845.

The Only Chief Executive to Have Fifteen Children

Letitia, Tyler's wife of twenty-nine years, died of a stroke in 1842. The fifty-two-year-old president and his family grieved and draped the White House in black. But after a period of mourning, Tyler began inviting family friends to spend quiet evenings at the White House. The David Gardiners and their beautiful twenty-two-year-old daughter, Julia, were among the old friends who often played cards with the president.

Julia, one of the most popular young women in Washington, had already turned down proposals of marriage from two senators and a Supreme Court justice. She was attracted to the tall, slender Tyler, who returned her interest, and before long the pair were quietly married in a church ceremony.

With the help of funds from the Gardiner family, Julia renovated the White House and bought some French furniture. She acquired a pet Italian greyhound, bought a fashionable wardrobe, and laid in some fancy French wines. Not only that, she planned to introduce a new dance, called the polka, at the next White House ball!

Although some people were shocked at the thirty-year age difference between Tyler and Julia, it was a real love match. The happy pair eventually had seven children. With eight from his first marriage, Tyler is the only chief executive to have fifteen children.

Tyler did not run for president again. When his term was over, he and Julia moved to Sherwood Forest plantation, the name he had given his retirement home in Virginia. (Tyler considered himself a political Robin Hood who liked to help the poor.) He set to work remodeling and enlarging the large clapboard house.

TYLER ESCAPES DEATH

On February 28, 1844, President Tyler, the members of his cabinet, members of the diplomatic corps, and members of Congress and their families took a cruise down the Potomac on the USS *Princeton*, a U.S. warship.

On the return trip, the officers fired one of the ship's big guns. It exploded and burst, sending shards of hot metal all over the deck. Several cabinet officers, seventeen seamen, and Tyler's black servant were killed. The father of Julia Gardiner also lost his life in the tragedy. President Tyler happened to be below deck, so he was not hurt.

☆ Visit ☆ SHERWOOD FOREST

Sherwood Forest still belongs to the Tyler family. It has been owned and occupied continuously by the Tylers, as a working plantation, for over 240 years. The house is three stories tall and only one room deep. At 300 feet in length, it still is known as "the longest frame house in America." Of special interest is the grave of Tyler's favorite horse. The inscription on the headstone reads, "Here lies the body of my favorite horse, The General. For over twenty years he bore me around the circuit of my practice, and in all that time he never made a blunder. Would that his master might say the same, John Tyler." There is also a family pet cemetery and a giant beech tree on which members of the Tyler family carved their initials.

You'll also enjoy seeing the haunted sitting room. Legend says that, at night, the Gray Lady floats down a hidden staircase to this room and rocks in a rocking chair that isn't there. At dawn the lady floats away. (Supposedly she is the only ghost who haunts a presidential home.)

Sherwood Forest is in Charles City, Virginia. Open daily, except New Year's Day, Thanksgiving, and Christmas, 9 A.M. to 5 P.M. Adults $7.50. Student discounts. For more information: Sherwood Forest Plantation, Box 8, Charles City, VA 23030. Telephone: 804-829-5377. Web site: http://www.sherwoodforest.org/

James Knox Polk

James K. Polk is often referred to as the first "dark horse" candidate for president. (At the racetrack, a "dark horse" is an unknown entrant that wins the race.) The Tennessean was so little known before the Democratic convention that voters kept asking, "Who is James K. Polk?" But Polk became one of the strongest, most successful presidents of the nineteenth century. In fact, he worked so hard that he was in a state of collapse by the end of his single term and died three months after leaving office at the age of fifty-three.

He Could Barely Drag Himself Around

James was born on November 2, 1795, in North Carolina. The eldest of ten children, he was often sick. His birthplace was a log cabin, but since his father was a prosperous cotton farmer, it was a "saddlebag" cabin: two log houses connected by a covered passageway.

When James was eleven, the family moved to Tennessee. It took six weeks to make the difficult 500-mile journey across the Blue Ridge Mountains and the Cumberland Plateau. Much of the time the family walked beside the creaking wagons that were loaded with their possessions.

By the time he was seventeen, James was so sickly he could barely drag himself around, and many times he was doubled over in pain. Finally a doctor found that the boy had gallstones and would not get better unless they were removed. In those days there were no anesthetics or antiseptics. If people lived through an operation, they often died from an infection. But James was courageous and determined to regain his health, so he had the operation and it was successful.

James's formal education did not begin until he was eighteen, but he did so well that his father, who was one of the richest men in the state, sent James to the University of North Carolina. The formerly awkward, shy young man excelled there and made many new friends. He joined the debate society and became a polished speaker. Legend says that James never missed a class the entire time he was at the university.

The Parties Lasted for a Full Week

James became a lawyer, and his first case was to defend his own father. Sam Polk had gotten into an argument with a man and punched him in the nose. The young lawyer presented such a good defense that the judge fined the elder Polk only a dollar. In gratitude, Sam built his son a law office and furnished it handsomely.

James began to court Sarah Childress, a pretty girl who was the daughter of a rich plantation owner. She was intelligent and well educated, and she had many admirers, but she chose James and they were married on New Year's Day in 1824. James and Sarah were so popular

Polk Parties

When Sarah Polk entertained at the White House, she was a gracious hostess, but she served no liquor. Since she also did not believe in dancing, the inaugural balls held for Polk were rather unusual. Until the presidential couple arrived to shake hands and greet their guests, people danced. The moment the Polks came, the music stopped and the dancers rushed to the sidelines. After shaking hands and chatting with their supporters, the Polks hurried to the next ball. The minute they left the building, the orchestra tuned up again and people spilled onto the dance floor once more.

that the wedding celebrations and parties lasted for a full week. The young couple began married life in a small house across the street from James's parents. Sarah was a devout Presbyterian who disapproved of drinking and dancing. Since the couple had no children, she focused her complete attention on helping her husband.

In 1823, Polk won a seat in the Tennessee House of Representatives. He became a well-known leader in the state and was called "Young Hickory" because he was such a loyal supporter of "Old Hickory," Andrew Jackson. Then in 1825, he was elected to the U.S. House of Representatives and served as its Speaker for four years. He left Congress in 1839 to become governor of Tennessee but served only one term.

Dark Horse

The Democrats favored Polk as Martin Van Buren's running mate in the election of 1844. But in a surprise move, when Van Buren's opponents blocked his nomination, dark horse Polk was selected as the Democratic candidate and went on to narrowly win the election.

Sarah Polk was more her husband's political partner than most First Ladies of the time. Early on, she told friends that if she and James ever lived in the White House, she "would never keep house and churn butter." True to her word, when Polk became president, she concerned herself with political issues. An avid newspaper reader, she always marked articles that she felt her husband should see. He relied on her opinion on most matters and paid attention to her suggestions. Although Sarah did not attend cabinet meetings, she was always present when officials came to see Polk at the White House. Sarah died in 1824, the first president's wife to die in the White House.

As president, Polk took on many difficult tasks, including acquiring California and the Oregon Territory. Polk's term in office was a stressful four years, which left the president exhausted. James died a little more than three months after leaving office in 1849.

White House Privacy

Even as early as the 1840s, presidential families have been concerned about the lack of privacy in the White House. Although the Polks had no children of their own, they often invited Joanna Rucker, a niece, to stay with them. The girl wrote to her family in Tennessee that she was often interrupted by strangers who slipped into the family's private quarters to have a look around, pretending to have lost their way to the president's office.

☆ Visit the ☆ POLK Ancestral Home

James K. Polk's ancestral home in Columbia, Tennessee, is now a historic site open to the public. The simple two-story, Federal-style house is built of handmade bricks. It is furnished with pieces the Polks used in the White House as well as those left by his parents. The house next door, which belonged to Polk's sisters and was always called "Sisters," is now the Visitors' Center.

One of the most unusual pieces of furniture in Polk's home is a round marble table with an eagle design made from small pieces of stone. Also of special interest is the "National Fan," which Mrs. Polk carried to the inaugural ball. On one side of the fan are ten small pictures of the preceding presidents, with "President Elect" written over Polk's likeness. On the other side is a rendering of the signing of the Declaration of Independence. Other popular items in the house are Sarah Polk's satin ball gown and the Bible upon which Polk swore his oath of office as president.

The Polk Ancestral Home is located at 301 W. Seventh Street, Columbia, Tennessee, about 50 miles south of Nashville. Open daily April through October, Monday through Saturday, 9 A.M. to 5 P.M., Sunday 1 P.M. to 5 P.M.; November through March, Monday through Saturday, 9 A.M. to 4 P.M., Sunday 1 P.M. to 4 P.M. Adults $5, senior citizens $4, children under 6 free. Student discounts. For more information: Polk Ancestral Home, Box 741, Columbia, TN 38402. Telephone: 931-388-2354. Web site: http://www.jameskpolk.com

Zachary Taylor

Zachary Taylor, our twelfth president, seemed an unlikely candidate for the nation's highest office. A career army officer who never lost a battle, he had little education, had never held office, and knew nothing about politics. In fact, when he was nominated as chief executive, he admitted that he had never even cast a vote. After becoming president, he lived only sixteen months.

Dressed in Buckskin, Denim, and a Coonskin Cap

Born in Virginia on November 24, 1784, Zachary was one of nine children. The family moved to a plantation of several thousand acres in Kentucky when Zachary was just a baby. As his father, a former army officer, prospered, the family's small log house was replaced by Springfield, a handsome two-story house.

Zachary loved the outdoors and explored the woods and fields dressed in buckskin, denim, and a coonskin cap like his hero and neighbor, the explorer Daniel Boone. Zachary's many friends were all welcome at Springfield, for his parents enjoyed visitors. Colonel Taylor was always happy to feed any growing boy who showed up at mealtime.

The Taylors at first taught their children at home; then they and their neighbors hired a teacher for the children of the area. Unfortunately, about all the schoolmaster taught Zachary was how to use a musket and a knife.

Later the boy was sent to an academy in Louisville, but he never became good at arithmetic or spelling. Reading was a different matter. He loved to read, especially war stories or books about soldiering and military tactics. His idea of a good time was listening to his father tell of his experiences in the Revolutionary War.

"Old Rough and Ready"

With Zachary's love of the military, it is not surprising that he joined the army. He chose the U.S. Infantry and entered as a private, but soon he rose to the rank of lieutenant. While stationed in New Orleans, he contracted yellow fever and nearly died. As soon as he was able to travel, he was given sick leave and returned home to Springfield for several months to recover. There, with good food, lots of rest, and loving care from his family, Zachary began to get well.

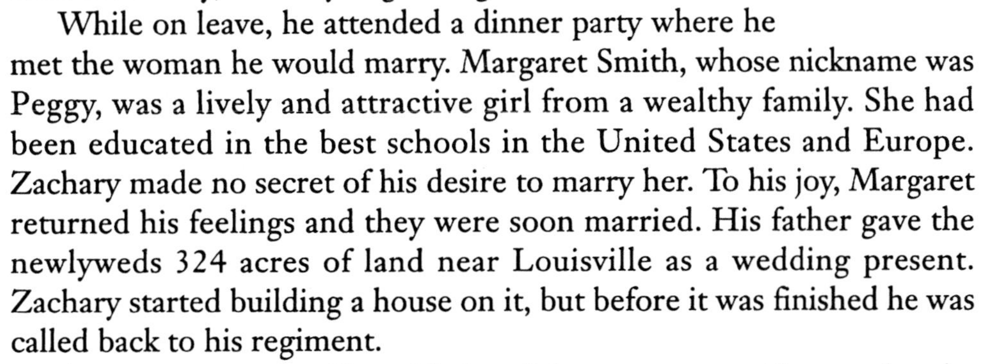

While on leave, he attended a dinner party where he met the woman he would marry. Margaret Smith, whose nickname was Peggy, was a lively and attractive girl from a wealthy family. She had been educated in the best schools in the United States and Europe. Zachary made no secret of his desire to marry her. To his joy, Margaret returned his feelings and they were soon married. His father gave the newlyweds 324 acres of land near Louisville as a wedding present. Zachary started building a house on it, but before it was finished he was called back to his regiment.

As a career army officer, Taylor did not wear a uniform unless he was posing for a picture. The rest of the time he wore an old straw hat and a shabby coat that had seen better times. Zachary Taylor was a strange-looking man. His large head and chest did not match his short legs and plump body. (Legend says that his legs were so short that he had to be boosted onto his horse by his orderly. Not only that, Taylor rode into battle with one leg hooked around the

WHITEY

When Zachary Taylor moved into the White House, Whitey, his favorite horse, accompanied him. Taylor was very attached to the animal that had carried him safely through many battles. The big white horse was allowed to graze on the White House lawn where the president could keep an eye on him. Following the president's death, Whitey followed his master's body in the funeral procession.

pommel of his saddle.) He was a kindly man, well loved by his troops. His lack of vanity, his down-to-earth manner, and his calm presence in battle won him the nickname of "Old Rough and Ready."

"I Regret Nothing"

In 1847, Taylor became a national hero after winning the battle of Buena Vista during the Mexican War, defeating the Mexican general Santa Anna. He was asked to be a candidate for president even before he returned from the battlefield. He later said that the idea "never entered my head, nor is it likely to enter the head of any sane person." But he finally accepted.

It was a bitter contest, but Taylor won the election. He took the news calmly, but his wife, Margaret, did not. She did not want to leave her home. In time, she did move to the White House, but the Taylors' daughter, Mary Elizabeth, acted as official hostess in her mother's place. At the White House, Margaret welcomed friends and family into the upstairs sitting room, presided at the family table, and went to church, but she took no part in formal social functions. Her years of traveling from post to post with her husband had worn her out. She was tired of making homes in "one God-forsaken place after another."

When Taylor was running for election, his political enemies had tried to find a reason to criticize him but did not dare because he was so popular. Instead, they attacked his wife, saying that she was an illiterate frontier woman who always carried a little sack of tobacco in her skirt pocket and smoked a corncob pipe. This was untrue. Margaret hated the habit of smoking so much that Zachary gave up cigars after he met her. Furthermore, she was always known as a "refined gentlewoman."

Taylor served only sixteen months of his term. After taking part in ceremonies at the Washington Monument on a blistering hot July 4 in 1850, he became ill. He lingered on the verge of death for several days. On the fifth day, he sat up in bed and announced, "I am going to die. I expect the summons very soon. I have tried to discharge my duties; I regret nothing, but I am sorry that I am about to leave my friends." He lay back down and in a matter of minutes, he was dead.

☆ Visit the ☆ ZACHARY TAYLOR National Cemetery

Today the only remaining house associated with Taylor is Springfield, his boyhood home. Unlike other presidential homes, it is privately owned and is not open to the public, but you can visit the burial site of Taylor and his First Lady in the Zachary Taylor National Cemetery in Louisville, Kentucky.

Although the mausoleum containing the two vaults is not large, the structure is beautiful. Built of limestone in the classic Roman style, the exterior is lined with marble and has double bronze doors with glass panels. Above them is the inscription, "1785 Zachary Taylor 1850." Since "Old Rough and Ready" was never a pretentious man, this simple burial place seems appropriate.

The Zachary Taylor National Cemetery is located at 4701 Brownsboro Road, 7 miles east of Louisville, Kentucky, on U.S. Highway 42. The gates of the cemetery are open at all times. The office is open daily, 8 A.M. to 4:30 P.M. Admission is free. For more information: Zachary Taylor National Cemetery, 4701 Brownsboro Road, Lousiville, KY 40701. Telephone: 502-893-3852.

Millard Fillmore

Millard Fillmore, our thirteenth president, was born in poverty, but he died a rich man. As president, he was considered a poor leader but an honorable man. The nation prospered during his presidency, since he believed that the government should promote business.

Millard Began to Educate Himself

Millard was born on January 7, 1800, in western New York. He spent his childhood on the frontier farm his parents leased in the woodlands. Even as a young child, he was expected to cut trees, clear land, hoe the crops, and help with the harvest. By the time he was thirteen, he was tall and husky and could do the work of a fully grown man.

If the boy took time to steal away to the woods to hunt squirrels, his father called him lazy. The elder Fillmore wanted Millard to become more successful than he had been. Since the farm was failing, Millard's father had him apprenticed to a clothmaker in New Hope, New York, when he was fourteen.

A public library opened in town when Millard was seventeen, and he began to educate himself. A couple of years later, he had a lucky break when an academy opened in New Hope. During the cloth mill's slack season, he enrolled in the school. He was hungry to learn and studying was a pleasure to him.

His parents were renting a farm from an elderly judge who heard about Millard's quick mind and desire to learn. The judge took Millard on as a law clerk until the mill opened again. The young man did a fine job and studied the judge's law books eagerly. When the mill opened, the old gentleman bought the grateful Millard's way out of the apprenticeship and set him to learning the practice of law.

Sometime later, the judge and Millard had a disagreement. The young law clerk moved on to Buffalo where he studied with other attorneys, then opened an office in the village of East Aurora. It seemed that Millard was still insecure because of his lack of education and preferred to begin in a small town until he built up his confidence. His business became successful and before long he was the most popular young bachelor in town.

Millard had had a special teacher, Abigail Powers, at the academy. The peppery red-haired young woman was twenty-one years of age when the nineteen-year-old Millard was in school there. He was attracted to her from the start, but she was the daughter of a prominent minister, the sister of a judge, and she had a good education herself. Millard was too unsure of himself to court her. Now that he was a prosperous lawyer, he began seeing Abigail again and they soon married. Later, they had two children, a son and a daughter. Abigail would become the first president's wife to have held a job before marriage.

A Fashionable Dresser

Abigail's belief in him gave Millard's confidence a boost and within a year, he was admitted as a counselor to the New York Supreme Court. He

Changes at the White House

During their time there, Abigail and Millard Fillmore modernized the White House. A cast-iron cooking stove was installed to replace the open hearth fireplace that had been used in the preparation of meals. Plumbers even hooked up a bathtub with running water.

Abigail established the first permanent White House library in the Oval Room. It is said that there was not a book—not even a Bible—in the house until the Fillmores moved in. Abigail had a personal library of more than 4,000 books, and after dinner, she and President Fillmore liked to sit in her library while their daughter, Mary Abigail, played the piano or harp.

gained the attention of prominent politicians and was elected to the New York State Assembly. Then in 1832, he won a seat to the U.S. House of Representatives and the Fillmores moved to Washington, D.C.

Fillmore became New York state comptroller (finance officer) in 1847. During that time, he was chosen to be General Zachary Taylor's running mate. While vice president, Fillmore, who was a fashionable dresser and wore a silk top hat, was said to look more like a president than Taylor, who was known for his sloppy dress.

President Taylor died suddenly in office in 1850 and Fillmore became president. He immediately announced in favor of the Compromise of 1850, a controversial set of bills concerning slavery. Although the compromise was intended to settle the slavery controversy, it only served as an uneasy truce.

In 1856, Fillmore ran for president again and was badly defeated.

☆ Visit the ☆ FILLMORE House Museum

Many of today's visitors are surprised to find that the Fillmore House Museum in East Aurora, New York, is such a modest frame house. Millard bought the dwelling when his first child was born. Eventually it was abandoned and stood in disrepair until 1930. A local artist bought the house and converted it to a studio. In 1875, the Aurora Historical Society purchased the residence and restored it as it was when the Fillmores lived there.

The Society's extensive research uncovered the original floor plan, interior details, and paint colors. These were combined with artifacts of the time and furniture of the period, some belonging to the Fillmore family. The museum also includes an interesting collection of antique toys.

The Fillmore House Museum is located at 24 Shearer Avenue, in East Aurora, New York, 20 miles southeast of Buffalo. Open Wednesday, Saturday, and Sunday, June through mid-October, 2 P.M. to 4 P.M. Adults $1, children free. For more information: Millard Fillmore House, Aurora Historical Association, Box 472, East Aurora, NY 14052. Telephone: 716-652-8875.

Franklin Pierce

Historians have called Franklin Pierce a "forgotten president" because he accomplished so little in office. One of the youngest presidents, taking office at the age of forty-eight, Pierce had been a well-loved public figure in New Hampshire when he left the state to assume the presidency. But when he returned home after only one term, the people of his town would not even give him an official welcome.

The Boy Became So Homesick He Ran Away from School

Franklin Pierce was born on a farm in New Hampshire on November 23, 1804. Shortly after his birth, the family moved to a large two-story house in town. His father, who had been a general in the Revolutionary War, kept a tavern where so many travelers stopped that the Pierce family always knew the political news of the nation.

Franklin attended a one-room school for a few years. He was such a good student that his father sent him to a nearby boarding school. The boy became so homesick he ran away from school and walked all the way home, a distance of more than 5 miles. When General Pierce saw his son, he greeted him pleasantly and told the boy to join the family for a big Sunday dinner. Franklin began to breathe easier; he was sure he would be allowed to remain at home. But after they

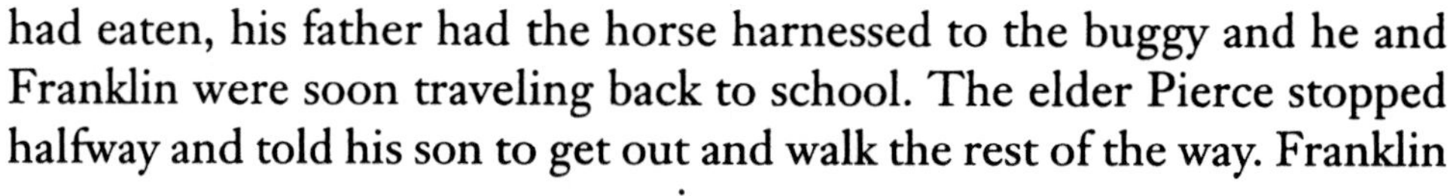

had eaten, his father had the horse harnessed to the buggy and he and Franklin were soon traveling back to school. The elder Pierce stopped halfway and told his son to get out and walk the rest of the way. Franklin never ran away again.

At Bowdoin College in Maine, Franklin was a popular and happy-go-lucky joker who had little time for study. His pranks often landed him in trouble, but somehow his grades were good enough for him to stay in school. In his junior year, he had an unhappy surprise: He had the lowest marks in his class. Embarrassed and angry, Franklin began studying and raised his grades. By the time he was a senior, he stood fifth from the top in his graduating class. His classmates included two of America's most famous writers, Henry Wadsworth Longfellow and Nathaniel Hawthorne.

A Tragic Personal Life

Following graduation, Franklin was appointed postmaster of his hometown. In his spare time, he studied law under a local attorney. By the time the young man passed the bar exam, his father had become the governor of New Hampshire. In 1829, the twenty-five-year-old Franklin was elected to the state legislature and then to the U.S. House of Representatives in 1832.

While a student, the handsome, fun-loving congressman had fallen in love with Jane Means Appleton, the daughter of the president of Bowdoin College. Shy and quiet, she was the opposite of the outgoing Franklin. Their first meeting was very romantic. Jane had been studying in the Bowdoin library when a thunderstorm came up. Seeing the flashes of lightning, she rushed out of the building. No sooner had she gotten outside than the thunder began to crack overhead. In terror she ran to a large oak tree and crouched against the trunk. Franklin, who had seen her leave the library, ran up to her and told her that she was in the worst possible place to be in a lightning storm. With that, he caught her up in his arms and carried her all the way home. They were married in 1834 and settled in Washington, D.C., where Franklin was serving in the House.

Franklin and Jane were to have a tragic personal life. She was frail and tubercular and she hated Washington politics. Later, two of their children died—one as an infant and the other at the age of four years. Two months before Pierce became president, their third son was killed in a train wreck before the eyes of his horrified parents. Franklin and Jane were devastated and she collapsed in grief.

Pierce meanwhile had been elected to the U.S. Senate. He served there until 1837, then returned to Concord to his law practice. When he returned to New Hampshire, Jane hoped he was through with politics. When the war with Mexico broke out, he volunteered and rode off to war on a prancing black horse. By the time the war was over, he was a brigadier general.

A Somber Inauguration

In 1852, Pierce became a compromise candidate for president (the party couldn't agree on any other nominee). Ironically, one of the reasons he had accepted was because he thought it would mean so much to his remaining child to be the son of the president of the United States.

Pierce assumed the presidency under the weight of the horrifying death of his last child. Over 80,000 people flocked to hear his inauguration speech, but it began to snow and only about 15,000 shivering spectators remained to the end. A reception followed at the White House, but the inaugural balls were canceled because Pierce was in mourning for his son. The grief-stricken Mrs. Pierce did not come to Washington for the inauguration but remained in seclusion at home.

Historians are convinced that the boy's tragic death affected Pierce's ability to govern. During Pierce's administration, the country moved one giant step closer to the Civil War.

Presidential Bodyguard

Franklin Pierce was the first president to have a full-time bodyguard. He assigned two men to police the White House South Lawn. Pierce had witnessed an attempt to kill Andrew Jackson and had lost another good friend who was killed in a duel over politics. Perhaps he was also feeling vulnerable because of his son's recent death.

☆ Visit the ☆ FRANKLIN PIERCE Homestead

The Franklin Pierce Homestead, built by his father the year Franklin was born, is a spacious two-story dwelling in Hillsborough, New Hampshire. The gracious old clapboard mansion surrounded by manicured lawns was restored by the New Hampshire Parks and Recreation Department in 1953.

Its large rooms, imported hand-stenciled wallpapers from France, fine furnishings, and ballroom that stretches the length of the second story are typical of the beauty and elegance with which the Pierce family surrounded itself. The house was also a gathering place of the great men of the state and nation.

The Franklin Pierce Homestead is located in Hillsborough, New Hampshire, 30 miles northwest of Manchester. Open June, September through Columbus Day, Saturday and Sunday only. Saturday 10 A.M. to 4 P.M., Sunday 1 P.M. to 4 P.M. July and August, Monday through Saturday, 10 A.M. to 4 P.M., Sunday 1 P.M. to 4 P.M. Additional open days: Memorial Day weekend, July 4, and September 5. Adults $2, children free. For more information: The Pierce Homestead, P.O. Box 896, Hillsborough, NH 03244. Telephone: 603-478-3165 or 603-464-5858. Web site: http://www.conknet.com/~hillsboro/pierce/homestead.html

James Buchanan

James Buchanan's fate was to become president on the brink of the Civil War. For decades, the turmoil over slavery and states' rights had been impossible to solve. Buchanan's attempts to please both the South and the North didn't satisfy either side. So happy was this chief executive to leave the White House, he told his successor, Abraham Lincoln, "If you are as happy, dear sir, on entering this house as I am on leaving it and returning home, you are the happiest man in the country."

He Was Soon Expelled

James Buchanan was born on April 23, 1791, during George Washington's presidency. His father ran a prosperous trading post at Cove Gap, Pennsylvania, until he sold it and moved his family to a large two-story brick house in the center of Mercersburg, Pennsylvania, where he opened a store.

From the time he was tall enough to see over the counter, James worked in the store. Customers were amazed that such a young child could add up the cost of their purchases. James had a quick mind and was extremely self-disciplined for a boy his age. He also excelled in reading and read every word of the local newspaper. But best of all, he loved to listen to the political talk around the potbellied stove in the store.

James left for Dickinson College when he was sixteen. He continued to get excellent grades, although he seemed to spend most of his time leading his friends on midnight drinking excursions around the campus. As a result of his behavior, he was soon expelled. James was sorry that he had embarrassed his family and asked for a second chance. He kept his word to do better by studying hard and avoiding the drinking parties. Following graduation, he returned home and studied law.

"I Feel That Happiness Has Fled from Me Forever"

After briefly practicing law, James was elected to the Pennsylvania House of Representatives. During this time he met Ann Coleman, the attractive daughter of a rich mill owner. The pair began to keep company, going for sleigh rides and attending parties and poetry readings. Before long they fell in love and became engaged.

Plans for the wedding were under way when rumors started that James had been seen with another woman. After Ann confronted him, he admitted that the stories were true. Hurt and angry, Ann broke the engagement and refused to see him again. She left to visit relatives in Philadelphia, where she died from an overdose of medicine. People said that she had committed suicide.

James was brokenhearted. He wrote Ann's family, begging to attend her funeral, but the letter was returned unopened. Anguished, he told his mother, "I feel that happiness has fled from me forever." Buchanan remained a bachelor for the rest of his life, the only president who never married. His niece, Harriet Lane, came to Washington, D.C., to act as White House hostess during his term. She became one of the most popular hostesses.

A Different Kind of Look

Buchanan was a handsome man who stood over 6 feet tall, with a high crest of white hair and blue eyes. But he carried his large head cocked to one side, which people said made him look a parrot. This tilted head was caused by poor vision—one of his eyes was farsighted and the other nearsighted.

In 1821, James was elected to the House of Representatives and served until 1831. When Andrew Jackson became president, he appointed Buchanan ambassador to Russia. Buchanan was reluctant to take the post because his mother was old, and he was afraid that she would die while he was out of the country. After much agonized thought, Buchanan left for St. Petersburg. As he had feared, his mother died while he was away.

After completing his work as ambassador, he returned to the United States and served in the

Senate for a decade. Following that he was appointed Polk's secretary of state and then Pierce's ambassador to Great Britain.

He Didn't Believe in Slavery

In 1857, at the age of sixty-five, Buchanan was elected the fifteenth president of the United States. The most important issue of the time was the widening gulf between the states over slavery. Although he didn't believe in slavery, Buchanan felt it should continue where it was already sanctioned by law. He held three fundamental convictions: that compromise was the only way a republic could survive, that citizens must obey the law no matter how unfair they thought it to be, and that questions of morality (as he called slavery) could not be settled by law. At the end of his term, he turned over to Lincoln a country that was still at peace, but Alabama, Georgia, Florida, Louisiana, Mississippi, South Carolina, and Texas had seceded from the Union over slavery.

☆ Visit ☆ WHEATLAND

James Buchanan was relieved to return home to Wheatland, his homestead on 22 acres of meadowland in Lancaster, Pennsylvania. He loved the elegant three-story, thirty-seven-room mansion. Although he was a bachelor, Buchanan did a great deal of entertaining there as he had done in the White House. He also had a large family of nieces and nephews who lived with him, so the redbrick house was well populated.

In 1936, the house and 4 acres of woodlands were restored by the James Buchanan Foundation. Today it is a Registered Historic Landmark. Guided tours are conducted by docents dressed in costumes of the period.

Wheatland is about 11.5 miles west of Lancaster, Pennsylvania. Open daily, except Thanksgiving, April through November, 10 A.M. to 4:15 P.M. Adults $5. Student discounts. For more information: Wheatland, 1120 Marietta Avenue, Lancaster, PA 17603. Telephone: 717-392-8721. Web site: http://www.lanclio.org/wheat.htm

Abraham Lincoln

The qualities that made Abraham Lincoln a great president were formed in early life. From his mother, he learned compassion, and both his parents set an example of honesty. His first teacher, who believed that slaves should be freed, influenced the boy's attitude toward slavery. Lincoln also never forgot the sight of slaves being driven past his family's log cabin like a herd of animals.

Abe Was Always Working

Abraham Lincoln was born on a farm in a crude log cabin with a dirt floor on February 12, 1809. He had one sister, Sarah, who was two years older, and a younger brother, who died at the age of two. When Abe was seven years old, the Lincolns were forced to leave their little farm. They headed for the Indiana frontier, where they carved a farm out of the wilderness.

Building a cabin, felling trees, and clearing the fertile land were backbreaking work. Abe, who was large for his age (he would grow to be 6 feet 4 inches tall), labored from dawn to dark and became skilled at using an ax. He was so good at splitting rails (logs) that he was later nicknamed "the Rail-Splitter." Since the family was poor and Abe was always working, he had little schooling.

When Abe was ten years old, his mother died. A year later, his father married a widow with three children. Sarah Bush Johnston brought love and warmth to the lonely wilderness family. She taught Abe to read and encouraged him to better himself, and he called her his "best friend in the world."

When Abe had a day off, he attended a one-room school, where he excelled in spelling, usually winning the "spell-downs" (spelling contests). Going to school was a rare treat, though, so Abe educated himself by borrowing books from neighbors.

"Dear Little Codgers"

When Abe grew older, he had many jobs. He was a deck-hand on a floatboat on the Illinois waterways, chopped wood, clerked in a store, surveyed land, was the post-master of New Salem, and fought in the Black Hawk War.

Later Abe began running a store. One day he bought a barrel filled with odds and ends. At the bottom of the cask he found a thick book called *Blackstone's Commentaries*, which has been described as the most important law book ever printed. After studying it night after night, he decided to become a lawyer. In 1834, he was elected to the Illinois House of Representatives.

Three years later, he joined the law office of John Stuart in Spring-field, Illinois. Stuart introduced Lincoln to Mary Todd, a quick-tempered young woman with blue eyes and curly brown hair. Abe fell in love with her, and they were married in 1842 and moved to Springfield.

The Lincolns had four sons, Robert, Edward (Eddie), William (Willie), and Thomas (Tad), but Eddie died when he was only four years old. Lincoln was a loving father who liked to spend time with his chil-dren. He was happiest when he sat in his favorite chair, watching the boys—his pet name for them was "dear little codgers"—romp on the floor around his long legs.

Walking on the Ceiling

One of the legends about Lincoln's childhood tells of the time his stepmother whitewashed the cabin ceiling. Joking about his height, she told Abe to keep his head clean so it wouldn't get the paint dirty. This gave him an idea. When she was out of the house, he grabbed a younger cousin who was wearing muddy shoes and held him upside down so that he left muddy footprints all over the ceiling. Mrs. Lincoln solved the puzzle quickly and enjoyed the joke, but Abe spent several hours helping her cover the grubby footprints with more whitewash.

"Now He Belongs to the Ages"

Legend says that Lincoln was popular with everyone but his wife. Mary nagged him about his "unrefined speech," was furious when he hurried to the door to admit visitors instead of waiting for the maid to do so, and sulked if he came to the dinner table in his shirtsleeves. When she ranted about his behavior being "common," Lincoln just smiled and agreed. He loved common people. In fact, he often said, "God, too, must love them, I guess, or He wouldn't have made so many of them."

In time Lincoln became a prosperous lawyer, known widely for his honesty and for his skill in the courtroom. He was also active in politics and was elected to the U.S. Congress. In 1854, Lincoln ran for the Senate. He lost that election, but in a series of debates against his opponent, Stephen A. Douglas, on the question of slavery, he gained national recognition, which won him a nomination for president in 1860.

Six weeks after Lincoln took office as president in 1861, Southern troops attacked Fort Sumter in South Carolina. The Civil War had begun. It was to be the bloodiest war in U.S. history, with the battles between the Union and the Confederacy raging for four years.

In February 1862, Willie and Tad came down with fevers. Tad got well, but Willie took a turn for the worse. The best doctors in Washington were called, but Willie died on February 20. Mary Lincoln was so grief-stricken that she could not attend her son's funeral. President Lincoln plunged into the worst gloom of his life. He and Willie had been especially close. People often said that the little boy was the one most like his father.

On January 2, 1863, Lincoln issued the Emancipation Proclamation, which declared the freedom of the 3 million slaves in the Southern states. Lincoln won reelection in 1864, and the Civil War finally ground to a halt in 1865. People in the North wanted to punish the defeated South, but Lincoln said that the Confederate states should be received back into the Union "with malice toward none, with charity to all."

Thieves Attempt to Steal Lincoln's Body

On November 7, 1876, a gang of thieves broke into Lincoln's tomb and partially pulled Lincoln's casket out. They planned to haul it away, bury it in the sand dunes of Indiana, and ask a $200,000 ransom for its return. One of the gang squealed to the Secret Service, however, and the rest of the group were arrested before they could get any farther. Since there was no penalty for such an offense, they were charged with breaking the lock on the tomb and were sentenced to a year in prison. The next legislature made body stealing a crime punishable by one to ten years' imprisonment.

On April 14, 1865, five days after the Civil War ended, Lincoln and his wife went to Ford's Theater to attend a play, *Our American Cousin.* During the third act, the well-known actor John Wilkes Booth crept into the theater box and shot Lincoln in the head.

The wounded president lived until the next morning. After his death, a cabinet member, speaking for the sorrowing nation, said, "Now he belongs to the ages." A train draped in black slowly carried the body of the fifty-six-year-old chief executive back to Springfield, Illinois, where he had lived the happiest years of his life.

✩ Visit the ✩ LINCOLN HOME National Historic Site

Today, Lincoln's home in Springfield, Illinois, is a National Historic Site and a part of four blocks restored by the National Park Service. The project created a historic district of the nineteenth-century neighborhood where the Lincolns lived for seventeen years. About fifty Lincoln-associated artifacts are on display in the home.

Abe bought the Greek Revival house for $1,500 (a year's salary in 1844) soon after the birth of his first son. To accommodate his growing family, he added more bedrooms. Much of the house remains the same today. Lincoln's stovepipe hat hangs in the hall, and the wallpaper chosen by Mrs. Lincoln still covers the walls. Lincoln's favorite rocking chair sits in a corner of the parlor, and his children's toys are scattered around their bedroom.

The city of Springfield features many other Lincoln attractions, such as Abe's law office, the family pew in the First Presbyterian Church, and the Old State Capitol Building where Lincoln served. The latter building contains the country's largest and most valuable collection of Lincoln's papers, documents, letters, and memorabilia.

Springfield, Illinois, is southwest of Chicago at the junction of I-55 and I-72. The Lincoln Home is open daily, except New Year's Day, Thanksgiving, and Christmas, 8:30 A.M. to 5 P.M. Admission is free. For more information: Superintendent, Lincoln Home National Historic Site, 413 South 8th Street, Springfield, IL 62701. Telephone: 217-492-4241. Web site: http://www.nps.gov/liho

Andrew Johnson

Andrew Johnson had been vice president for only forty-one days when Lincoln was assassinated. Johnson, our seventeenth president, is mainly remembered as the first president who was accused of misconduct in office and impeached, although he was later acquitted. Johnson thought of himself as a defender of the poor and oppressed. Many scholars feel that both blacks and whites would have suffered less if Johnson's plans for rebuilding the South had been followed after the Civil War.

Never Had a Day of Formal Schooling

Johnson was born on December 29, 1808, to a poverty-stricken family living in a dirt-floored shack in Raleigh, North Carolina. His father died when the boy was three years old, making times even harder for Mrs. Johnson and her children.

Schools cost money, so Andy never had a day of formal schooling. At the age of fourteen, he and his older brother were apprenticed to a tailor and became what was known as "bound boys," working for their room and board while they learned the trade of tailoring. Andy was not particularly interested in the trade, but he did like one thing about it. Workmen in the shop took turns reading or hired readers to entertain them while they stitched. They listened to novels, biographies, newspapers, sermons—anything available. Studying until late every night, Andy learned to read, although he still could not write. His favorite book was a collection of famous political speeches.

Andy and his brother became skilled tailors. They ran away and set up their own tailor shop in South Carolina, but when Andy was seventeen, the two returned home to find their mother and stepfather nearly starving. Determined to make a better life for his family, Andy bought a broken-down old horse and a rickety two-wheel cart. The boys piled their possessions on the cart and helped Mrs. Johnson climb on top of the load. With the men walking behind, the family headed for Tennessee.

Andy again opened a tailor shop and was soon successful enough to buy a farm for the family in Greenville, Tennessee. He met and married a local girl named Eliza McCardle. The tall, pretty sixteen-year-old turned out to be a clever businesswoman and a good manager. She also taught Andy how to write and do some arithmetic. The Johnsons would have five children, two girls and three boys.

A Powerful Speaker

By the time he was twenty-three, Johnson was one of the area's most respected tradesmen and was mayor of the town. He went on to serve as a state legislator, as a congressman, as governor of Tennessee, and as a U.S. senator. He was known as a powerful speaker who paid little attention to manners, style, or grammar.

During most of Johnson's time in the House of Representatives and the Senate, Eliza, who was not well, remained at the family home in Greenville, Tennessee. Their older daughter, Martha, who was attending

A Fixer Upper

When the Johnsons moved into the White House, the place was a shambles. Following Lincoln's assassination, curious sightseers had invaded the White House and helped themselves to souvenirs, leaving torn curtains, filthy carpets, and broken furniture. Congress appropriated $30,000 for repairs, which everyone said was not enough. People were impressed, however, at how good the mansion looked after Martha Patterson had finished the renovation.

Mrs. English's Seminary for Young Ladies in Washington, D.C., acted as her father's secretary and hostess on weekends.

When Tennessee seceded from the Union in 1861, Johnson sided with the North because he believed that secession would be bad for the whole country. He was the only southern legislator left in Washington D.C. President Lincoln appointed him military governor of the Union-controlled territory of Tennessee, then later urged delegates to nominate Johnson for vice president.

Tactful, Johnson Was Not

Following Lincoln's assassination, Johnson assumed the presidency. It was one of the most difficult times the country had ever seen. The nation needed a man of tact to deal with the opposing North and South. Tactful, Johnson was not.

Johnson did his best, including coming up with a plan called "Reconstruction" to put the union back together, but he did not have Lincoln's power to persuade people. Johnson fought with Congress over how Reconstruction should be carried out. In 1868, the House of Representatives voted to impeach the president, although Johnson had not committed a crime; he had merely disagreed with Congress. He was later found innocent by one vote in a Senate trial.

During Johnson's time in office, Eliza was in such poor health that she rarely came downstairs at the White House. An avid newspaper reader, Eliza reported the day's news to her husband each evening. If the news was bad, she waited until the next morning to tell him about it, so that he would sleep well. Although the president and his wife were such different personalities, they were said to be very fond of each other.

Their daughter, Martha, her husband, Tennessee Senator David Patterson, and their two children moved into the White House, where Martha acted as her father's hostess. The Johnsons' other daughter, Mary, a widow with three children, also came to live at the White House, along with twelve-year-old Andrew Johnson, Jr.

Johnson finished out his term and went home to Tennessee in 1869. But he returned to Washington in 1875, as a senator. Some of the senators who had

Andy's Polar Bear Garden

One of Andrew Johnson's greatest achievements was the purchase of Alaska. With the president's guidance in 1867, Secretary of State William Seward arranged for the United States to buy the region from Russia. In those days most people considered the 586,400 square miles of land a wasteland covered with nothing but snow and ice all the time. Everybody thought it was crazy to pay $7.2 million for the unexplored territory and called it everything from "Seward's Folly" to "Andy's Polar Bear Garden." Later, when gold was discovered in the Klondike, they decided the purchase was a bargain!

voted to remove him from office had come to admire Johnson's courage, and when he entered the Senate, they stood and applauded him.

He died later that summer and was buried in Greenville, Tennessee. As he had requested, his body was wrapped in the Stars and Stripes and a copy of the Constitution was placed beneath his head.

☆ Visit the ☆ ANDREW JOHNSON National Historic Site

The town of Greenville, Tennessee, has earmarked several locations associated with Andrew Johnson. The National Historic Site's Visitor Center contains his tiny early tailor shop within its walls and still holds some of the original furnishings and tools he used. The center also contains exhibits, letters, and displays that trace the career of one of this country's most unusual presidents.

Across the street is the small, two-story brick house where the Johnsons lived when they were newly married. Several blocks away is the three-story house Johnson bought when he grew more prosperous and in which he lived until his death. Two of its most interesting furnishings are a hand-carved ivory basket given to Johnson by Queen Emma of Hawaii, and a table made of 500 small pieces of wood, presented by the people of Ireland.

A mile up Main Street on the summit of Signal Hill is the Andrew Johnson National Cemetery, where the former chief executive is buried. His resting place is marked by a tall marble shaft topped with an eagle. His epitaph reads, "His faith in the people never wavered."

Greenville, Tennessee, is 70 miles east of Knoxville. The site is open daily, except Christmas, 9 A.M. to 5 P.M. Adults $2. Student discounts. For more information: Andrew Johnson National Historic Site, P.O. Box 1088, Greenville, TN 37744. Telephone: 423-638-3551. Web site: http://www.nps.gov/anjo

Ulysses Simpson Grant

Although many people believe that Ulysses S. Grant was the most capable general in the Civil War, few thought much of him as a president. His administration was tainted by scandal. Grant himself was probably not involved in the wrongdoing. He simply had no talent for politics and held little control over the people he appointed to office.

Above All Else, He Loved Horses

Our eighteenth president was born on April 27, 1822, in Point Pleasant, Ohio, the oldest of six children. His father was a tanner of hides, and his mother was a quiet, religious woman. A year after Ulysses' birth, his father moved his business to Georgetown, Ohio.

Named Hiram Ulysses at birth, he was later misregistered at West Point as Ulysses Simpson Grant. Rather than tell anyone about the mistake, he decided to go by that name. He liked it better than his own because the initials of his old name spelled out "Hug," a nickname he was stuck with during his childhood.

The shy youngster was an average student, although he had a special talent in mathematics. But above all else, he loved horses. When he was three or four years of age, he would swing by the tails of strange horses, weave through their legs, or crawl under the bellies of the family carriage team. By the time he was five, he could ride standing on a horse's back like a circus performer. Before long, neighbors were hiring him to train their riding horses. The boy would vault onto one of the animals, grab its mane, and cling like a flea to the running, bucking horse until it became tame.

Ulysses entered the U.S. Military Academy at West Point when he was seventeen years old. In a letter he wrote home, he described the pants of his uniform as "tight to my skin as the bark to tree, and if I do not walk military—that is, if I bend over quickly or run—they are very apt to crack with a report as loud as a pistol."

While at West Point, Ulysses met fellow cadets William Tecumseh Sherman and George McClellan, young men with whom he would later serve during the Civil War, and Cadet Thomas "Stonewall" Jackson, whom he would face as the enemy. Grant would say that knowing these men's strengths and weaknesses helped him in battle. In all, fifty of his classmates fought with or against him in the Civil War.

Upon graduation, Lieutenant Grant was posted to Jefferson Barracks in St. Louis, Missouri. On a visit to the family of a West Point friend, Ulysses met the man's seventeen-year-old sister. No romantic sparks flew until he discovered that Julia Dent was an accomplished horsewoman. That caught his interest and the two began taking long horseback rides. They fell in love, became engaged, and were married after Grant returned from the Mexican-American War.

Commanding General of All the Armies

Julia and the couple's young son stayed with her parents while Ulysses' army career took him from the jungles of Panama to California. Grant, lonely for his family, began to drink heavily. He was forced to resign and returned home in disgrace to try farming, which was also a failure.

Horses at the White House

After becoming president, Grant had new stables built at the White House to accommodate his high-stepping team. Once, he was arrested for speeding on the streets of Washington, D.C., but no charges were pressed when the police found that he was the president. When a friend from back home asked Grant how he liked being president and living in the capital city, he replied that he would enjoy it a lot more if he had a good road on which to race his horses.

But after the Civil War started, officers were in short supply. Grant joined the Union Army with the rank of colonel. Abraham Lincoln, desperate for higher commanding officers, commissioned him as a brigadier general. Grant's determination, tactics, and skills helped bring victory to the Union. By the war's end, he was commanding general of all the Union armies. This time he did not come home in disgrace—he returned a national hero.

Grant Was a Trusting Man

Grant was extremely popular. People longed for national unity, and they thought he could bring that about. In 1858, every Republican party delegate voted to nominate Grant. Unfortunately, Grant was not the man for the job. He had no idea of the duties or powers of the presidency and didn't seem to understand the changes that were happening in the aftermath of the Civil War.

Grant was a trusting man who was probably brought down by his friends, not his enemies. As he said in his last message to the nation, "my failures were errors of judgment not of intent." Leading officials whom he appointed were involved in railroad scandals, tax corruption, and Indian agency frauds. His private secretary and trusted friend, General Orville Babcock, was a member of a group who defrauded the government of its taxes on liquor.

Although his administration was scandalous, Grant achieved some good during his terms of office. He held the country together during the rebuilding of the South, and he harassed Congress until they passed the Civil Rights Act of 1875, designed to protect the rights of the newly freed slaves.

Jesse's Dogs

The Grants' youngest son, Jesse, had several dogs. One by one, they got sick and died. The boy was so brokenhearted that President Grant called a meeting and announced that everyone on the staff would be fired if another of the boy's dogs died. From then on, Jesse's dogs stayed healthy.

"The Happiest Days of My Life"

Unlike many First Ladies, Julia Grant said that her years at the White House were "the happiest days of my life." With the Grant family in residence, the mansion became the social center of Washington, D.C. Julia loved giving elegant dinner parties. Ulysses was not as fond of the social life as his wife was, but he humored her.

Two of the Grants' four children were adults by the time their father became president. Ten-year-old Jesse, the family clown, soon became one of the most popular boys who ever lived at the White House. He consulted his father's cabinet when he had a problem and they usually solved it! To be sure he was never lonely, Mrs. Grant invited six other boys to visit Jesse regularly. They formed a secret club and met in a gardener's toolshed on the White House grounds.

Nellie, probably her father's favorite, was thirteen when the family went to live in the White House. Nellie was the first young girl to live in the White House in twenty-five years. The American public treated the teenager like a princess and gobbled up every word printed about her!

Following his final term, Grant and his wife set sail to see the world. The pair traveled to Europe and the Orient, visiting heads of state. Wherever he went, Grant received a warm welcome. After returning to the United States, they moved to their home in Galena, Illinois, for a few months and then relocated to New York.

☆ Visit ☆ Grant's Tomb

Ulysses S. Grant died on July 23, 1885, at the age of sixty-three. According to his wishes, he was buried in New York City. His body was escorted to its final resting place by a parade of thousands of Civil War veterans. The funeral was one of the most impressive ever held in the city.

The General Grant National Memorial, known simply as Grant's Tomb, is located on Riverside Drive in New York City. The picturesque burial site, on a bluff overlooking the Hudson River, was chosen by the former president's son. Built of solid white granite, it is a combination of classical architectural styles, with large columns across the front, massive bronze doors, and a rotunda on top. Between two sculptured figures are carved the former general's famous words, "Let us have peace."

Inside, resting beneath the domed rotunda, are two 12-foot, 9-ton, black marble sarcophagi (stone coffins) where Grant and his wife, Julia, are entombed. Bronze busts of some other Civil War heroes, and of some allegorical figures, stand between the arches. Two small rooms contain Civil War mementos, photographs, and other items that relate to Grant's life and career.

Grant's Tomb is in Riverside Park at Riverside Drive and West 122nd Street in New York City. Open Wednesday through Sunday, 9 A.M. to 5 P.M. Admission is free. For more information: Superintendent, General Grant National Memorial, 26 Wall Street, New York, NY 10005. Telephone: 212-666-1640. Web site: http://www.nps.gov/gegr/index.htm

Rutherford Birchard Hayes

After the troubled Grant administration, Rutherford Hayes, the nineteenth president, seemed a breath of fresh air. He was hardworking and honest, and so were the men he chose to work for him. Most historians say this red-haired, blue-eyed chief executive was an above-average president who left the office in far better shape than he found it.

A Household of Women

Born on October 24, 1822, in Delaware, Ohio, Hayes was a sickly baby whose mother was afraid he would not live. Neighbors who stopped by in the morning got in the habit of asking if the baby had died during the night. "Rud" (his childhood nickname) survived, but he was a thin and weak child.

His father had died ten weeks before his birth, and his younger brother drowned at the age of two, leaving the boy to grow up in a household of women who worried about almost every breath he took. His older sister, Fanny, was devoted to him, but no matter how hard Rud tried, she urged him to achieve more. Historians have said that his "extreme nervousness," which lasted well past his teenaged years, may have been due to his mother and Fanny's overprotection.

Hayes received a good education for the time. He went to Harvard Law School, then opened a law practice in Fremont, Ohio, the home of his uncle Sardis Hayes.

After five years, he moved to Cincinnati, where his business flourished and he married Lucy Webb. Lucy was a spirited young woman who fought for women's rights, especially the right to vote.

Hayes Won by One Vote

During the Civil War, Hayes was appointed to the rank of major in the 23rd Ohio Volunteer Infantry. He was wounded five times and rose to the rank of major general. In 1864, while still in the army, he was elected to Congress but refused to take his seat until the war was over and the Union had won. A few years later, he became governor of Ohio. His victory in the presidential election in 1876 was a close one. The dispute over the winner was taken to Congress, who argued about it for months. Finally both sides agreed to a special commission to decide the question, and Hayes won by one vote.

Lucy Loved Children

Of the Hayeses' eight children, all but six-year-old Fanny and nine-year-old Scott were grown up when Hayes became president. The two children were fascinated by many of the White House guests. The visit of Chief Red Cloud, a Sioux Indian, was exciting for Scott, especially when the chief patted him on the head and called him "a young brave."

Lucy, the first president's wife to graduate from college, was a gracious hostess. She was also known as one of the most kindhearted of all

President Hayes Plays a Joke

Although President and Mrs. Hayes did not serve alcohol in the White House, rumors started that waiters were supplying rum-filled oranges to their guests. People joked that this stage of the state dinners was called "the Life-Saving Station." But Hayes had the last laugh. He wrote in his diary, "The joke was not on us but on the drinking people. My orders were to flavor [the oranges] with the same flavor that is found in Jamaica rum. This took! There was not a drop of spirits in them."

the First Ladies. Lucy loved children. She began the Easter Egg Roll on the White House lawn that is still held to this day. Strong-minded but sweet-tempered, she was also a believer in temperance and allowed no alcohol to be served in the White House. (People gave her the nickname of "Lemonade Lucy" while she was First Lady.)

Hayes, who served from 1877 to 1881, is remembered for his efforts to heal the wounds of the Civil War. His presidency also established several firsts. He was the first president to take the oath of office in the White House rather than in the Capitol. Since people expected trouble over the close election in 1876, the inauguration ceremony was private. Hayes was the first to have a telephone and a typewriter while in the White House, and he was the first chief executive to travel to the West Coast during his term in office.

Hayes left the White House in 1881 and retired to his estate, Spiegel Grove, saying, "Nobody ever left the Presidency with less regret than I." He completely withdrew from politics, but he worked to improve conditions in prisons, to help veterans receive their pensions, and to provide education for all.

In 1893, at the age of seventy, he became ill while visiting in Cleveland. He insisted on going home, saying, "I'd rather die in Spiegel Grove than anywhere else." On January 17, he got his wish. He is buried on the grounds of his home in a peaceful tree-shaded knoll, near what was once a famous Indian trail running from Lake Erie to the Ohio River.

Visit of Thomas A. Edison

In April 1878, Thomas A. Edison, a thirty-one-year-old inventor, was invited to the White House. The young man had just been granted a patent on his phonograph and President Hayes was eager to see and hear the machine. It is said that the demonstration was a big success, for the inventor did not leave until 3:30 A.M.!

☆ Visit the RUTHERFORD B. HAYES Presidential Center ☆

Rutherford B. Hayes was the first president to have a library and museum created to house his personal papers after leaving office. Unlike future presidential libraries, which would be overseen by the National Archives and Records Administration, the Rutherford B. Hayes Memorial Library and Museum was established by the Hayes family and the Ohio Historical Society. Opened on May 30, 1916, the center's site is the wooded 25-acre Hayes estate, Spiegel Grove, in Fremont, Ohio.

Guided tours are conducted through the sprawling, twenty-room, redbrick Victorian mansion. There is also more than a mile of winding trails on the wooded estate, which is enclosed by a decorated wrought-iron fence with six gates brought from the White House. During his first year in office, Hayes began naming the trees in Spiegel Grove after famous people. The custom continued after his death. William McKinley, James Garfield, Grover Cleveland, and General William Sherman have trees named for them. When President Taft, a large man who weighed 300 pounds, visited the Hayes estate, he chose the biggest oak tree he could find for his namesake!

Some especially popular exhibits at the Hayes Library are the military weapons used by General Hayes during the Civil War, the elaborate dollhouses of the president's daughter, the president's carriage, and the special china that Lucy chose for the White House. Lucy had commissioned a young woman to paint a set of dishes showing the plants and animals of North America, from ferns to cactus, raccoons to wild turkeys. Some people said the china was as ugly as it could be, but a Maine senator's wife told friends that it was worth a trip from New York to Washington just to see a state dinner set with the dishes.

The Rutherford B. Hayes Presidential Center is in Fremont, Ohio. Open Monday through Saturday, except New Year's Day, Thanksgiving, and Christmas, 9 A.M. to 5 P.M. Adults $7.50. Student discounts. For more information: Presidential Center, Spiegel Grove, Fremont, OH 43410-2796. Telephone: 419-332-2081. Web site: http://www.rbhayes.org

James Abram Garfield

James A. Garfield, who was assassinated after only four months in office, was familiar with every detail of state and national government long before he became president. For twenty years he had served as a state senator and a congressman. It's been said that had he never been elected president, he still would have earned a place in U.S. history for his distinguished service in Congress.

The Last President to Be Born in a Log Cabin!

James was born on a farm in Orange Township, Ohio, on November 19, 1831, the last president to be born in a log cabin! His father died of pneumonia two years later after fighting a forest fire near his home. After her husband's death, Mrs. Garfield ran the family farm with her four children.

Mrs. Garfield seemed to favor young James and hovered over him constantly. The little boy was bright, and his mother never let him forget that he was destined for great things. Since the local school was too far away for him to attend, Mrs. Garfield persuaded neighbors to build a school on her land.

Mrs. Garfield remarried, but she soon divorced her second husband. Divorce was rare in those days and James was deeply affected.

Other children teased him about not having a father. Although he was intelligent and made good grades, he didn't get along well with other people, and he often had blinding headaches, chronic throat and chest infections, and stomachaches. When he stayed at home sick, he escaped into books, especially books about the sea and sailing ships.

By the time the boy was seventeen, he wanted to become a sailor. Against his mother's wishes, he left home to become a seaman. Unfortunately, the first captain he approached looking for work was drunk and laughed the boy off the ship. Stung by this rejection, James got a job on an Erie Canal boat and turned out to be a good worker.

But he nearly drowned three times and contracted malaria, so James returned home. His mother talked him into going back to school. This time he was well liked by his peers and teachers.

When James was twenty-seven years of age, he married Lucretia Rudolph, a dark-eyed beauty who had loved him for a long time. James later confessed that he had been married for four years before he fell in love with his wife. When he did, though, he became a devoted husband to "Crete." The Garfields would have seven children, of whom five would live to adulthood.

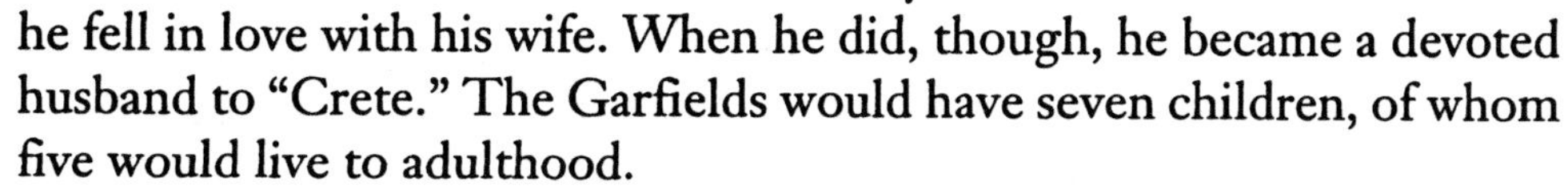

A "Front Porch" Campaign

Garfield worked his way up to president of Western Reserve Eclectic Institute (now Hiram College). In 1859 he became a state senator in Ohio. During his time in office, the Civil War began and Garfield marched off to fight with the Union Army as a lieutenant colonel. He led his men through some of the war's most horrible battles, and by the time peace was declared, he had risen to the rank of major general through his bravery.

After the war he was elected to the U.S. House of Representatives, where he served from 1863 to 1880. In 1880, Garfield was nominated as the Republican candidate for president. In those days, presidential hopefuls did not do much campaigning for office; instead their friends made speeches on their behalf. Garfield's backers urged him to "sit cross-legged and look wise until after the election," so he returned home to Mentor, Ohio. There he conducted a "front porch" campaign, a term used in those days for giving speeches and answering the questions of people who came to the candidate's home. It was a close election, but Garfield won, becoming our twentieth president.

Hit by Two Bullets

He plunged into office with great plans for the next four years. He selected his cabinet, began laying the foundation of a strong foreign policy in South America, and launched an investigation of the Post Office.

The Garfields were a cheerful family and moved into the White House with high hopes. Although Lucretia did not especially enjoy the social duties of the White House, she was very hospitable and her dinners and twice-weekly receptions were popular.

Irvin, the Garfields' youngest son, was an athletic child. A visitor waiting for the president was amazed to see the boy ride his high-wheeled bicycle down the grand staircase without falling. The instant Irvin reached the first floor, he zipped past the openmouthed stranger and careened into the East Room, "the spokes of his wheel flashing like the tail of a comet." Horror-stricken visitors and servants stood with their backs pressed to the wall as Irvin then whizzed round and round the historic room.

By summer, the busy president was looking forward to some time off. He planned to travel to Williams College, in Massachusetts, where he would enroll two of his sons and then attend his twenty-fifth class reunion. Following that, the whole family would vacation at the seashore. It looked to be a fine summer for all.

On July 1, 1881, the newspapers announced that the president would be leaving Washington, D.C., from the Baltimore and Potomac Railroad Station the next day. The following morning, as Garfield walked through the station, he was shot by a mentally unbalanced man who had unsuccessfully sought a federal appointment. The assassin later said that God told him to kill Garfield.

Presidents were not well guarded in those days, so no one shielded

The Bedsprings Interfered

When President Garfield was shot, there were no X-ray machines, but Alexander Graham Bell had invented an electric metal detector, which he brought to Garfield's bedside. He ran it over the president's body, checking to see if the remaining bullet had punctured some vital organ, but he could not tell because the metal bedsprings under the mattress affected the metal detector.

him. Later it was found that the short, bearded Charles Guiteau had been following the president for days, seeking just the right opportunity to kill him.

Garfield was hit by two bullets, but he was not dead. His wounds would not be considered all that serious today, but so many doctors had poked at them with dirty fingers and unsterile instruments that they became infected. Since there were no antibiotics, the infection could not be halted and Garfield died on September 19, 1881. Elizabeth Garfield, the president's mother, who had always feared something awful would happen to her son, witnessed his assassination.

☆ Visit the ☆ James A. Garfield National Historic Site

Today, Garfield's home in Mentor, Ohio, has recently been renovated by the National Park Service. The house was part of a small farm that Garfield bought so that "my boys can learn to work and where I can get some exercise, where I can touch the earth and get some strength from it." The thirty-room Victorian mansion with gables and bay windows was dubbed "Lawnfield" by the mob of reporters who camped there during Garfield's "front porch" campaign for the presidency in 1880.

The Lawnfield library is filled with the president's books, souvenirs, and gifts. Included are Garfield's congressional desk and a funeral wreath from Queen Victoria of England. One of the most interesting objects in the room is the president's desk, which has 122 compartments!

The James A. Garfield National Historic Site is located at 8095 Mentor Avenue, Mentor, Ohio 44060. Open daily, except New Year's Day, Martin Luther King Day, Thanksgiving, Christmas Eve, and Christmas Day, Monday through Saturday 10:00 A.M. to 5:00 P.M., Sunday noon to 5:00 P.M. Adults $6, senior citizens $5, children 6–12 $4, children under 6 free. For more information: Site Manager, James A. Garfield National Historic Site, 8095 Mentor Avenue, Mentor, OH 44060. Telephone: 440-255-8722. Web site: http://www.nps.gov/jaga/index.htm

Chester Alan Arthur

When Vice President Chester A. Arthur was swept into the presidency following James Garfield's assassination, the nation was amazed and uneasy. Some suggested that Arthur reject the presidency, for they considered him a political hack, without national or foreign policy experience. But to everyone's surprise, he rose to the challenge as our twenty-first president and served the nation honorably.

He Still Had Time for Fun

Born on October 5, 1829, in North Fairfield, Vermont, Chester was the fifth child of a Baptist minister. The family often moved to new towns and the Reverend Arthur taught his children at home. In some ways the constant moving was hard, but it taught Chester and his eight brothers and sisters to make friends easily.

When he was fifteen years old, Chester entered a private school to prepare for college. Here, he developed two new interests: literature and politics. At Union College he studied hard, was elected to Phi Beta Kappa (the national honor society), and served as president of the debate club, but he still had time for fun. Once Chester and his friends dumped the school bell in the Erie Canal. He also sometimes joined his friends in one of their most dangerous pastimes, jumping on and off trains that were pulling into the local station.

Upon graduation from college, he taught school and studied to become an attorney in his spare time. He moved to New York and began working at an established law firm.

At twenty-six years of age, he met Ellen Herndon, the nineteen-year-old cousin of a friend. Ellen was a talented musician from a wealthy family in Virginia. Although her parents did not want their daughter to marry a struggling young attorney, the pair became engaged and married a few years later.

Chester was just another striving young lawyer until he argued an important case in 1855. He represented Lizzie Jennings, a black woman who, because of her color, was forced to leave an all-white streetcar in Brooklyn. He won monetary damages for his client, and as a result of the trial, racial segregation of public transportation in New York City was soon ended. This important case brought Arthur a lot of good publicity and public attention.

During the Civil War, Arthur served in the New York State Militia as a brigadier general. Although he never saw combat, he was quartermaster general of the militia, arranging food, lodging, transportation, and supplies for the state's troops.

Ousted from Office by President Hayes

Because of his army experience and thanks to influential friends, Arthur was appointed collector of the customshouse in the port of New York. In that capacity he passed out jobs to thousands of Republicans, and although he was personally honest, he closed his eyes to some criminal activities in his office. As a result, he was ousted from office by President Hayes. Most people thought this disgrace would finish Arthur's political career, but two years later in 1880, he was nominated as the Republican vice presidential candidate on the ticket with James Garfield.

That same year, Arthur's wife, Ellen, died at the age of 42, leaving a son and a daughter. Arthur was deeply sentimental about his wife and had a bouquet of fresh flowers placed in front of her portrait every day.

Although many people were upset that Arthur had become vice president, an article in the *Nation*, a magazine devoted to reform, actually said that he could do little harm in the vice presidency, since he would probably never become president. After all, President Garfield was a healthy man and seemed to have no enemies. Little did they know! Garfield was killed 200 days after taking office and by September 22, 1881, Chester A. Arthur was president of the United States.

"Living Above the Store"

President Arthur did not move into the White House for three months for two reasons. He didn't want to rush the grief-stricken Mrs. Garfield out of her home and, in any case, the White House was badly in need of renovation. Arthur, who prided himself on his sense of style, decided to decorate the mansion himself. He had twenty-four wagon-loads of furniture and household goods carried away. Some of these things were junk, but others dated back to John Adams's administration and were historically priceless. Arthur had them sold at auction and used the money for new furnishings.

The president was not thrilled about "living above the store." He considered it a bad idea to live in the same house where you did business. In fact, he told a reporter, "You have no idea how depressing and fatiguing it is to live in the same house where you work."

Arthur's sister, Mary Arthur McElroy, was his official hostess. He tried to keep his children out of the public eye, so they would not be pestered by the press or by curiosity seekers. "Little Nell," his daughter, who was only nine when her father became president, seldom appeared in public.

Arthur loved all the fine things that money could buy. He had a personal valet who took care of his clothes and helped him dress. Arthur enjoyed wearing fashionable clothes and had at least eighty beautifully tailored suits. It was said that he changed his clothes several times a day. He rode in an elegant, green-leather-trimmed carriage pulled by magnificent horses wearing blankets sporting his initials.

A Big Fish Story

Chester Arthur was one of the finest fishermen in the country and caught many large trout, salmon, and other fish. He was often photographed enjoying the sport wearing a three-piece suit, white shirt, and tie. One day when he was fishing off the coast of Rhode Island, he hooked an 80-pound bass, one of the largest fish ever seen in that region.

To people's surprise, Arthur's administration was honest, and he filled his cabinet with competent men. He continued to defend the rights of minorities, as he had in the Lizzie Jennings case, by supporting civil rights for African Americans.

Arthur hoped to be elected in his own right in 1884. Although people felt he had done a good job, Republican leaders were not behind him, so he was not nominated. He left Washington, D.C., and returned to his law practice and private life in New York City. He died two years later, a man who had redeemed himself and served his country well.

☆ Visit the ☆ CHESTER A. ARTHUR Historic Site

The Chester A. Arthur Historic Site in Fairfield, Vermont, consists of a replica of the parsonage (a house furnished to a minister by his church) where he was born. The tiny house has two downstairs rooms and a sleeping loft. Instead of furnishings, it has pictorial exhibits of Arthur's life and political career. Just down the rocky hill stands the Baptist church where the Reverend Arthur preached. A plain little brick building, it never had electricity.

The Chester A. Arthur Historic Site is in Fairfield, Vermont. Open June through mid-October, Wednesday through Sunday, 9:30 A.M. to 5:30 P.M. Admission is $1. For more information: Vermont District for Historic Preservation, 133 State Street, Drawer 33, Montpelier, VT 05633-1201. Telephone: 802-828-3211. Web site: http://www.cit.state.vt.us/dca/historic/hpsites.htm

Grover Cleveland

Grover Cleveland was both our twenty-second and twenty-fourth president. Although he had little education and almost no political experience, historians consider him to have been a good chief executive. Honest and independent, he was a man of strong character, determined to do what was right regardless of what others said. At a time when many politicians were busy getting rich, Cleveland had the good of the nation at heart.

Grover Was Ambitious

Stephen Grover Cleveland was born on March 18, 1837, in Caldwell, New Jersey, a middle child with eight brothers and sisters. His father was a Presbyterian minister who was paid only a small salary. The family moved to Clinton, New York, when Grover was a boy. Grover started doing odd jobs to help out while he was still in grammar school. Whether it was painting a fence, cleaning a carriage, or helping the boatmen on the Erie Canal, he worked hard and tried his best. Grover was determined to make something of himself. He dropped "Stephen" from his name because he felt that "Grover Cleveland" sounded more distinguished.

Young Grover hated Sundays. He had to attend Sunday school,

followed by two long church services. After church he and his brothers and sisters were not allowed to play, since their father said the Sabbath (Sunday) was meant for rest and prayer.

At least one time, Grover rebelled. He and some friends crept into the open schoolhouse at midnight and began ringing the big bell. When the townspeople heard the noise, they hurried into the street to see what was happening. The boys had planned to be long gone by this time, but they'd accidentally locked themselves inside the building. They could do nothing but wait to be caught and punished by their parents.

Although Reverend Richard Cleveland was a graduate of Yale, Grover did not get a good education. His father died when Grover was sixteen, and he had to quit school and take a job in a general store. He roomed with another boy and slept in a rope bed with a straw mattress.

When Grover was eighteen, he and a friend headed west, where job opportunities were said to be better. Grover got only as far as Buffalo, New York, the home of his uncle. He planned to leave the next day, but the man offered him a job paying $10 a month, plus a room and food. The offer was too good for him to refuse.

Grover's uncle also arranged for him to study law at a local law office. The attorney had never seen a law clerk try as hard as Grover did. He studied for hours each day, ran errands, helped prepare simple cases, and worked late every night.

Sickened by the Whole Experience

By the time he was twenty-two, Grover had become a member of the law firm, but he was still not satisfied. He became interested in politics and ran for district attorney, but he lost the race.

Grover next ran for sheriff of Erie County. He won, but he found himself in an uncomfortable position. Local party leaders tried to get him to hire people who were not qualified. Grover also found dishonest contractors who were cheating the county. He cleaned up the office as much as possible but was sickened by the whole experience and did not run for a second term.

In time, he became mayor of Buffalo and then governor of New York. His reputation for honesty and hard work followed him in every job he held. Even before he was sworn in as governor, people were saying Grover Cleveland would be a fine Democratic presidential candidate in 1884.

They Even Interrupted His Honeymoon

Cleveland won a close race for president in 1884. He entered the White House as a bachelor of forty-seven, but in April 1886 he became engaged to twenty-one-year-old Frances Folsom, the beautiful daughter of his old friend and former law partner. Those who saw Frances and her mother, Emma, visiting the White House were surprised because they thought the president was interested in the older woman, a widow who was nearer his age.

Cleveland was the only president to be married at the White House. Only a few relatives and officials were invited, although a large crowd gathered outside the mansion to cheer Cleveland and his new bride. Frances wore a white silk gown with a 15-foot train and a bridal veil fastened to her hair with orange blossoms. As the ceremony ended, all the church bells in the city rang and a twenty-one-gun salute was fired from the nearby naval yard. An elaborate wedding supper was served in the White House dining room, where the guests toasted the bride and groom with champagne.

People were excited about Frances becoming the youngest First Lady in U.S. history. Newspaper reporters and photographers followed the couple everywhere. Cleveland finally grew angry when they even interrupted his honeymoon.

BABY RUTH

When the Clevelands moved back to the White House for his second term, their second daughter was seventeen months old. Her name was Ruth, but everyone called her Baby Ruth. (Many people claim that the candy bar was named after the little girl.) President Cleveland, like George Washington and Andrew Jackson, believed that the White House belonged to the nation, so many people poured through the mansion. Those visitors enjoyed holding and playing with Baby Ruth. Legend says that one day the tiny girl could not be found. The frantic family started a search, covering every inch of the great house. Baby Ruth was finally found with a group of people touring the White House. She seemed to be enjoying herself, but it is said that President Cleveland put an end to the "open-door policy" after that!

The first child of a president to be born in the White House was Esther Cleveland. When a reporter asked her what she remembered about living there, Esther said she recalled sitting in the downstairs hall pulling on a pair of gloves because it was moving day. When someone asked her why she was leaving, she answered, "Because McKinley's [the next president] coming, and there can't be two presidents."

Although it has been said that few men were as unprepared for the presidency as Grover Cleveland, he was fearless and independent. He began restoring honesty to government. He was one of our hardest-working presidents and often remained at his desk until two or three in the morning.

Both of Cleveland's presidential terms were marked by countless battles with Congress over the tariff system that placed large duties on goods from other countries entering the United States. He used the veto (presidential power to kill a law that legislators have already passed) more often than the combined twenty-one presidents before him.

☆ Visit the ☆ Grover Cleveland Birthplace Historic Site

The Grover Cleveland Birthplace Historic Site is located at 207 Bloomfield Avenue, in Caldwell, New Jersey. The simple frame two-and-a-half-story building, which was built in 1832 for the sum of $1,490, is typical of many houses of the period, with a gabled roof and clapboard siding.

At this time the Grover Cleveland Birthplace is undergoing renovation. Special reservations are necessary for viewing the house until it is finished. For more information telephone: 973-226-0001

Benjamin Harrison

Benjamin Harrison was the son of an Ohio congressman, the grandson of the ninth president of the United States, and the great-grandson of a signer of the Declaration of Independence. Inaugurated 100 years after George Washington, he was known as the "Centennial President." Independent, highly intelligent, and having a strong sense of justice, he has been said to have been a greater man than he was a president.

"The Pious Moonlight Dude"

The second of ten children, Ben was born on August 20, 1833, in North Bend, Ohio, and grew up on his grandfather's farm. The boy helped with farm chores, fished, and hunted ducks and squirrels. He loved the outdoors and grew strong and muscular although he was only 5 feet, 6 inches tall. (When he ran for the presidency, cartoonists drew him as a tiny figure nearly hidden under a huge beaver hat.)

Ben's father built a one-room log schoolhouse and hired a tutor for the Harrison children and their cousins. Ben, who was a serious boy, worked hard at his studies and loved to read. He especially enjoyed reading his grandfather's books. One of the boy's favorites was *Ivanhoe,* by Sir Walter Scott, which he read over and over again.

He went to prep school, then to Miami University in Oxford, Ohio, known as the "Yale of the Midwest." Ben joined a fraternity, was active in a debating society, and made good grades, but he still found time for romance.

He had met Caroline Lavinia Scott, the daughter of a Presbyterian minister, in prep school. Benjamin spent so many evenings on the preacher's front porch, courting the man's daughter, that his friends called him "the pious moonlight dude." The pair became secretly engaged.

By the time Ben finished college, he had decided to enter politics. At the age of nineteen, he began to study law and apprenticed with an attorney in Cincinnati. But he missed Caroline so much he went back to his hometown to finish his law studies, and they were married in 1853.

He set up his law practice in Indianapolis and became a successful attorney. Ben had a pleasing courtroom manner and was skilled in cross-examining witnesses. He soon got into politics as Republican state secretary, but his political career was interrupted by the Civil War.

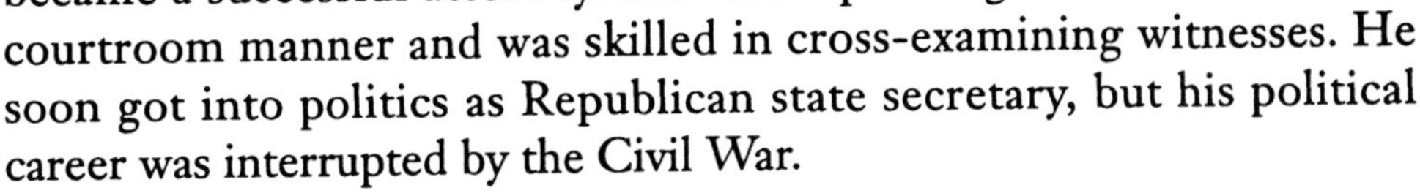

"Little Ben"

Harrison commanded the 70th Indiana Regiment and led his men through battle after battle. He became a hero because of his bravery and by the end of the war, he was a brigadier general.

Following the war, he was elected senator from Indiana. Then, in 1888, he ran against Grover Cleveland for president. Harrison conducted a "front porch" campaign from his broad verandah. More than 300,000 people paraded past his house during this period, stopping to listen as "Little Ben" (about the worst thing the Democrats said about Harrison) gave speeches and asked for their votes.

Harrison won the close election with 49 percent of the vote to Cleveland's 48 percent. The new president moved into the White House with his extended family, which included the Harrisons' daughter, Mary Harrison McKee, and her two children, Mrs. Harrison's ninety-year-old father, and her widowed niece. The house reverberated with life. (Once during Harrison's time in office, one of the president's grandchildren had scarlet fever and the whole White House was quarantined!) To get a respite, the president sometimes had his high-stepping Kentucky thoroughbreds harnessed to his dark green coach and, taking the reins from his coachman, drove along the streets of Washington, D.C., in the cool of the evening, enjoying the peace and quiet.

Mrs. Harrison tried to enlarge the White House while she was there, but Congress balked at spending the money, so she made do with a general cleanup and other minor improvements. She also found that there wasn't enough of the same china pattern to serve a state dinner. An accomplished artist, the First Lady worked with a designer to produce a set of dishes decorated with corn tassels, forty-four stars symbolizing the states, and an American eagle representing strength and unity.

But some people said the White House was dull during the Harrison administration. There was little entertaining and few glamorous dinner parties. The Harrisons considered themselves plain people who went to bed early and kept regular hours. They were the first to have electricity in the White House, but they never quite figured it out and may have been a little afraid of it. Legend says that for a long time they did not turn on the lights in their bedrooms or push the electric bell because they were afraid of getting shocked.

As president, Harrison had several important laws passed and expanded the U.S. Navy, but he served only one term. In 1892 he lost the election to former president Grover Cleveland. He returned home to Indianapolis alone, since Caroline had just died of tuberculosis. He busied himself practicing law. In time, he remarried. His second wife was the first Mrs. Harrison's niece who had lived with them in the White House. Although his grown children objected to the marriage, Mary and Benjamin led a happy life until his death from influenza at the age of sixty-seven.

Old Whiskers

The Harrisons always had lots of pets, including dogs, horses, and a possum, but their favorite was a goat named Old Whiskers. Harrison's grandchildren often hitched the animal to a small cart to pull them around the White House grounds. One day when the gate was open, the goat made a dash for freedom. Pulling the cart with the excited children aboard, Old Whiskers darted through the opening and headed down Pennsylvania Avenue. President Harrison saw what was happening and chased after the careening cart, goat, and grandchildren, dressed in his top hat and frock coat, waving his cane and yelling "Stop, stop." Nobody was hurt, but onlookers saw a new side to the president that day!

☆ Visit the ☆ BENJAMIN HARRISON Home

Benjamin Harrison's sixteen-room house in Indianapolis is a National Historic Landmark. The handsome brick mansion with rambling upstairs and downstairs porches is surrounded by a large lawn. Ten rooms have been restored with many of the Harrison family's furnishings. Also on display is the china designed by Harrison's first wife, Caroline, for the White House.

The Harrison Research Library is on the third floor, as are exhibits that focus on his presidential career. Of special interest among the family items is a one-horse open sleigh built of wood with chrome trim.

The Benjamin Harrison Home is in Indianapolis, Indiana. Open daily, except New Year's Day, Easter, Indianapolis 500 Race Day, Memorial Day, Labor Day, Thanksgiving, Christmas Eve, and Christmas Day, Monday through Saturday 10 A.M. to 3:30 P.M, Sunday 12:30 P.M to 3:30 P.M. Adults $2.50. Student discounts. For more information: Benjamin Harrison Home, 1230 N. Delaware Street, Indianapolis, IN 46202. Telephone: 317-631-1898. Web site: http://www.surf-ici.com/harrison/

William McKinley

William McKinley felt that the president should follow the will of the people. His critics said that he was not a good leader, but few presidents have had a stronger character than this twenty-fifth chief executive. He was an honest and gentle man who reached out to help anyone in need, even the man who assassinated him. After the assailant had fired two bullets into McKinley's body, McKinley gasped to nearby guards, "Don't let them hurt him." Four decades later, Harry Truman said, "You might find a better leader, but you'd have to look a long way to find a better man."

Lucky Seven

Born on January 29, 1843, in Niles, Ohio, William was the seventh of nine children. When he was born, the proud father was said to have exclaimed, "Lucky seven!" He named the boy for himself, William McKinley, Jr.

William was a good student who learned quickly and got along with other children. He especially enjoyed playing "soldier" and was good with a bow and arrow.

At the age of seventeen, William enrolled in Allegheny College. He promised his parents that he "would study every hour he was not eating, sleeping or in class." He must have done that, for he broke down under the strain and had to return home to regain his health. When he was well enough to go back, his family no longer had the money for him to finish school.

William got a job in the local post office, then went off to serve in the Union Army. He fought in the Battle of Antietam, the bloodiest battle of the Civil War, in which more than 20,000 soldiers were killed or wounded. He rose through the ranks to become a major, known for his courage and leadership. After witnessing the horrors of war, he determined to work for peace. Following the war, he apprenticed with a practicing attorney and opened a law office. Soon, McKinley was courting the daughter of the town's leading banker.

Ida Saxon was a proud and high-spirited girl who had a mind of her own. She had toured Europe and when she returned home, she became a cashier in her father's bank. On a moonlight carriage ride, McKinley proposed. Later he told friends, "Surprising enough, the foolish young girl accepted." They were married and remained devoted to each other the rest of their lives, although Ida later suffered from poor health and was seldom seen at public affairs. The couple had two daughters, but they died young, one as an infant and the other at the age of four.

"I Have No Enemies"

At thirty-four, McKinley became one of the youngest members of Congress and in time was one of its most effective lawmakers. In 1891 he was elected governor of Ohio. While governor, McKinley became known for his devotion to his invalid wife. Each morning after leaving their hotel, he would pause beneath Ida's window and bow to her before hurrying off to work. And every afternoon at three o'clock, he would stop whatever he was doing, hurry to his office window, and wave his handkerchief at his wife, who was sitting across the street in their hotel suite.

By 1896, he was running against Democrat William Jennings Bryan for the presidency. People thought the ever-courteous McKinley had little chance against the vibrant Bryan, but McKinley conducted a vigorous "front porch" campaign from his home in Canton, Ohio. To most people's surprise, McKinley won the election.

A little over a year after McKinley's inauguration, the United States went to war with Spain over Cuba. The Spanish-American War was short and by December, a peace treaty with Spain had been signed. As a result the United States bought Puerto Rico, Guam, and the Philippines for $20 million. The United States also annexed the Hawaiian Islands during McKinley's administration.

In 1901, McKinley easily won a second term. Then on September 6, he traveled to Buffalo, New York, to open the Pan-American Exposition. The president's advisers had warned him against mingling with so many people at close range, but McKinley said, "I have no enemies."

Leon Czolgosz, a twenty-eight-year-old unemployed mill worker, was waiting in line to shake hands with the president. Mentally unbalanced, he later said that he wanted "to kill a ruler." Unfortunately, nobody noticed that Czolgosz held a gun concealed by a handkerchief. As he came face-to-face with McKinley, he fired two shots through the handkerchief. The president collapsed to the floor. As he was helped to a nearby chair, McKinley gasped to his secretary to be careful how his wife was told about the shooting. He was then rushed into surgery and it looked as if he would recover, but he died of infection eight days later.

A Red Carnation

Journalists said the "pale, short, and purposeful" McKinley resembled a young Napoleon. He always wore a red carnation in his buttonhole and kept his glasses on a black cord around his neck. Legend says that McKinley had just bent down to give a little girl the carnation from his buttonhole when he was assassinated.

☆ Visit the ☆ McKINLEY National Memorial and Museum

The slain president was laid to rest in Canton, Ohio. Today, the McKinley National Memorial is one of our most impressive presidential burial sites. One hundred and eight broad steps rise to the handsome pink granite building with double domes. Mrs. McKinley and their two little daughters also lie in the grand mausoleum, whose exterior dome soars 95 feet into the air.

The McKinley Museum of History, Science, and Industry is at the foot of the stairs below the memorial. It includes a gallery devoted to the former president, his clothes, photographs, furniture, and personal mementos. One of the most interesting exhibits is a scene of the cheery McKinley living room, featuring lifelike wax figures of the McKinleys in formal evening clothes, looking as if they were waiting for guests to arrive for a party. A Street of Shops contains full-size reproductions of typical stores of an Ohio town of the 1880s. Discover World, devoted to hands-on science, and a planetarium are also part of the attractions dedicated to McKinley.

The McKinley National Memorial and Museum is in Canton, Ohio. Open daily, except Easter Sunday, Memorial Day, Labor Day, Thanksgiving, Christmas Eve, and Christmas Day, Monday through Saturday 9 A.M. to 5 P.M., Sunday noon to 5 P.M. During June, July, and August, hours are extended to 6 P.M. Adults $5. Student discounts. For more information: McKinley Museum, 800 McKinley Monument Drive, Canton, OH 44703. Telephone: 330-455-7043. Web site: http://www.mckinleymuseum.org/

Theodore Roosevelt

Theodore Roosevelt, our nation's twenty-sixth president, was probably the most active president this country has ever known. Just short of forty-three years old when he assumed office, "Teddy" Roosevelt served the nation with gusto and seemed to enjoy each day he spent in office, calling the presidency a "bully pulpit." He was so energetic, some people said he reminded them of a steam engine in trousers!

A Great Outdoorsman

Teddy was born on October 27, 1858, in New York City, the second of four children of a wealthy banker. As a child, Teddy suffered with nearly fatal asthma attacks. Doctors tried everything to cure him, including having the frail child smoke cigars, which made him vomit. It seemed that after throwing up, his breathing eased. Many nights he slept sitting in a chair to prevent him from coughing and gasping for breath all night.

When he was about twelve, he began to work out with weights and became very muscular. But one day when he was riding a train, two other boys began teasing him about his thick glasses, upper-class accent, and "fancy" clothes. Finally, he could stand it no longer and started swinging at the two. Although Teddy was strong, he did not know how to fight and lost badly.

When his father found out about this humiliating experience, he arranged for Teddy to take boxing lessons at a local gym. He took to the sport quickly, but he did not neglect his education.

Young Teddy was also a naturalist. Passing a fish market one day, he saw a dead seal laid out on a slab. Fascinated, he went in to examine it more closely. The next day he went back with a tape measure. He measured the seal and wrote the dimensions in a notebook. Eventually the market owner gave him the skull, and Teddy put it in a "museum" that he and his cousins had put together, which included dead mice, bones, and rocks.

What finally cured Teddy's asthma was a trip to the West. He spent months in the Rockies, riding horseback, camping out, and sleeping under the stars. From then on Teddy was a great outdoorsman, never happier than when he was astride a horse, sailing a boat, or hiking cross-country.

In 1876, Teddy entered Harvard. He talked so much in one class that the professor said, "Look here, Roosevelt, let me talk. I'm running this course." During his time at Harvard he also met the love of his life, Alice Lee. He proposed to her on Valentine's Day in 1880 and they were married. But soon tragedy struck. Alice Lee died of a kidney disease, leaving a baby daughter they had also named Alice. The same day his wife died, Roosevelt's mother succumbed to typhoid fever.

Reeling from the double loss, Roosevelt left the baby in the care of his sister and headed West. He bought a ranch in the Dakota Territory, where he spent nearly every waking hour in the saddle. He remained there for two years. Once more, the West proved good medicine for Roosevelt, and he pulled his shattered life together. He returned to the East and married Edith Carow, who had been a childhood friend. She came to love baby Alice and the couple started a new family in New York City.

The Rough Riders

In October 1886, Teddy ran for mayor of New York City, but he was defeated. President Harrison appointed him a Civil Service commissioner. Next, Roosevelt became New York City police commissioner, then assistant secretary of the navy. During the Spanish-American War, he formed and commanded the Rough Riders, the First U.S. Voluntary Cavalry Regiment, which included both cowboys from the West and adventurous polo-playing horsemen from the East. The regiment's finest hour came when Teddy led his men on a wild charge up San Juan Hill in Cuba. Everyone except the officers had been forced to leave their horses in Florida, so most of the men scrambled up on foot. Years later, Teddy would declare, "San Juan was the greatest day of my life." After the war he became governor of New York, and then U.S. vice president in 1900.

The Father of Our National Parks

When William McKinley was assassinated, Roosevelt became president and served out the slain chief executive's term. He was elected for another four years in 1904. He was the first president to use government to solve social problems, making laws that improved working conditions. In 1906 he became the first American to win a Nobel prize (a prize awarded yearly in areas such as medicine, science, and literature) when he won the Nobel Peace Prize for his part in ending the Russo-Japanese War. Roosevelt was also our first conservation-minded chief executive. He started programs to save wilderness areas and is the father of our national parks system.

A "White House Gang"

Not only did Roosevelt leave his mark on the White House, so did his six children. People said they were the rowdiest kids who ever lived there! Having inherited their father's sense of mischief, they were always up to something. They climbed the flagpole, organized their friends into a "White House gang," and dropped snowballs from the balconies onto the heads of policemen below. Stilt-walking and roller-skating on the polished floors were two of their favorite activities. One of their more quiet games was sliding down the elegant staircases on cookie sheets. Once they even put their pony in the White House elevator for a ride.

Alice, Roosevelt's oldest daughter, was the leader in many of these escapades. She was high-spirited and as full of fun as her father. Alice had a snake named Emily Spaghetti, and she took the pet along when she went visiting, nearly causing a riot among her friends' families. Washington society buzzed with tales of her "hair-raising shenanigans." One day, after witnessing one of these capers, Owen Wister, a close friend of the family, asked Roosevelt why he didn't curb some of Alice's mischief. Roosevelt answered with good humor, "Listen, I can be president or I can attend to Alice."

Following his time in office, Roosevelt returned to private life at Sagamore Hill, a rambling house on New York's Long Island. The estate was nearly a zoo, with many pets, including a herd of ponies and a one-legged rooster. The house resounded with the voices of children, as well as Roosevelt's friends, prizefighters and professors, foreign leaders and local politicians.

TEDDY BEAR

Roosevelt once traveled to the Mississippi-Louisiana border to settle a boundary dispute. While there, his hosts arranged for him to go bear hunting. Although the president hunted high and low, not a bear was to be found. It looked as if Teddy would have to return to the capital without a trophy.

So eager were his hosts to see that the president bagged a bear, they found a bear cub, tied it to a tree, and then directed the hunting party to the spot. When Roosevelt saw the bear, he ordered it cut loose, saying he would never shoot an animal that did not have a chance to escape.

A political cartoonist who was along on the trip drew a picture of Roosevelt saving the cub's life. A Brooklyn couple saw the picture and made a cuddly toy that looked like the cartoon bear. With Roosevelt's permission, they called it Teddy's Bear, which eventually evolved into the teddy bear, the most popular soft toy of all time.

☆ Visit ☆ Sagamore Hill

The twenty-three-room turreted house in Oyster Bay, New York, is furnished with original Roosevelt pieces. Although far from beautiful, the house looks comfortable and cozy. Downstairs, one of the most interesting rooms is Roosevelt's study, which is paneled in mahogany, swamp cypress, hazel, and black walnut. Filled with books, paintings, flags, and hunting trophies, the room reflects Roosevelt's colorful personality and many interests.

On the second floor is a bathroom with a great porcelain bathtub. Theodore junior remembered that the tub made gurgling noises as the water drained out. "We were told by our Irish nurse that these were the outcries of the 'faucet lady' and we watched with care to see if we could catch a glimpse of her head in the pipe."

As you stroll the landscaped grounds and prowl the halls of Sagamore Hill, it's easy to imagine the joyous father and his brood at work and play. No wonder Roosevelt said, "At Sagamore Hill we love a great many things . . . birds and trees and books, and all things beautiful and horses and rifles and children and hard work and the joy of life."

Sagamore Hill is in Oyster Bay, New York. Open daily, except New Year's Day, Thanksgiving, and Christmas, 9:30 A.M. to 4:30 P.M. (5:30 P.M. in summer). Admission is $2. For more information: Sagamore Hill National Historic Site, Oyster Bay, NY 11771. Telephone: 516-922-4447 or 516-922-4788. Web site: http://www.nps.gov/htdocs4/sahi/index.htm

William Howard Taft

"I'll be glad to be going; this is the loneliest place in the world," said William Howard Taft at the end of his presidential term in 1913. The twenty-seventh president of the United States was an effective administrator but a poor politician. Easygoing, he had little use for the hardships of political life and spent four uncomfortable years in the White House.

A Firm Believer in Women's Rights

Willie was born on September 15, 1857, in Cincinnati, Ohio. He was good-natured and plump, and he had a dimple in one cheek. Folks said baby William looked like a cherub in a painting.

The Taft household was a happy and lively one with six children and one set of grandparents all living together. The family spent many nights around the fireside, reading aloud, popping corn, or playing chess. The Taft children learned good manners from their parents, who treated people with courtesy and expected their children to do the same. Willie's father was a judge who later became secretary of war under President Ulysses Grant.

Although Willie was an excellent student, he never took himself too seriously. He liked to play baseball and was a good second baseman. He also enjoyed playing tennis, skating, swimming, and taking dancing lessons. Many boys hated dancing class, but Willie enjoyed it. (He was always a good dancer and light on his feet, even when he was extremely overweight in later years.)

In high school, Will dated the prettiest and the most intelligent girls, who seemed to enjoy his company and polite ways. They also may have appreciated the fact that unlike most men and boys of the time, he was already a firm believer in women's rights.

Like his father and brothers, Will went to Yale. When he graduated, he returned to Cincinnati to study law. On a sledding party he met eighteen-year-old Helen "Nellie" Herron. Her father was a well-to-do-lawyer and a partner of Rutherford Hayes, who later became president.

Although women did not get the vote for another forty years after the young couple met, Nellie was an emancipated young woman. She didn't hide the fact that she was unusually intelligent, and she spoke her mind without hesitation. Early on, she decided that she would only marry a man who would treat her as an equal. It took Will five years to win her.

The Tafts adored each other through the years and had a strong and happy marriage. He always called her "a treasure" and vowed that she was smart enough to be a cabinet member. Nellie called him "that adorable Will Taft" and relished the challenge of making a home for him and their three children in Manila, Japan, China, and other places he was sent by the government.

Throwing Out the First Ball

Taft served on the Ohio Supreme Court in 1887 and was appointed as the first governor of the Philippines in 1901. Both Taft and Nellie enjoyed their time there and were extremely popular with the Filipino people. (Taft, who by then weighed nearly 300 pounds, had his own bathtub shipped to his new post.)

When Theodore Roosevelt became president of the United States, he convinced Taft to become his secretary of war. This led to Taft's election to the presidency. "I always said it would be a cold day when I got to be president," Taft joked to Theodore Roosevelt when a winter storm descended on Washington on Taft's inauguration day in 1909.

As president, Taft supported a federal income tax and established the Department of Labor. New Mexico and Arizona became the forty-seventh and forty-eighth states during Taft's administration. Taft also started the tradition of the president throwing out the first ball of the baseball season.

The Tafts kept a milk cow named Pauline while they were in the White House. The cow grazed all over the White House lawn as well as on the grounds of the Executive Office building next door. Legend says that although the Tafts enjoyed the fresh milk Pauline gave, the White House gardeners weren't too pleased with the way the cow nibbled the shrubs and messed up the lawns, especially when they were getting the place ready for one of Nellie's Shakespeare productions on the grounds!

Nellie Taft loved being the First Lady and was a brilliant hostess. During the four years of grand social events she staged at the White House, the most outstanding was an evening garden party for several thousand guests on the Tafts' silver wedding anniversary. Nellie later wrote in her book, *Recollections of Full Years*, that it was "the greatest event" in her White House experience.

The Tafts' children, who were already adults when their father was president, went on to become well-known people: Their daughter, Helen, became dean of Bryn Mawr College; their eldest, Robert A. Taft, became a leading senator; and their younger son, Charles P. Taft II, was mayor of Cincinnati.

Washington Cherry Trees

In 1909, Mrs. Taft had 80 Japanese cherry trees planted along the banks of the Potomac River. Then in December, 3,000 more trees arrived in Washington, D.C., as a gift from the city of Tokyo. These same trees are still visited by thousands of people each spring when they bloom magnificently.

Taft served but one term, then went back to Yale University as a law professor. But his sweetest dream came true when President Harding appointed him the tenth chief justice of the U.S. Supreme Court in 1921, a post he held until 1930. He died a month after retiring at the age of seventy-two, the only man in U.S. history to have headed two branches of the federal government.

☆ Visit the ☆ WILLIAM HOWARD TAFT National Historic Site

William Howard Taft's birthplace and family home is located atop a hill in the Mount Auburn section of Cincinnati, Ohio. The large, two-story, yellow brick house, built in the elegant Greek Revival style, is set on a sweeping lawn surrounded by an ornamental wrought-iron fence.

The historic site has been restored to look as it did when Taft lived there as a child and young adult. The ground floor is fully furnished with many of the Taft family's belongings, including family portraits, furniture, and books. The upper floor contains a museum, galleries, and exhibits that highlight Taft's career as a lawyer, college president, governor of the Philippines, president of the United States, and chief justice of the Supreme Court.

The William Howard Taft National Historic Site is in Cincinnati, Ohio. Open daily, except New Year's Day, Thanksgiving, and Christmas, 10 A.M. to 4 P.M. Admission is free. For more information: Taft National Historic Site, 2038 Auburn Avenue, Cincinnati, OH 45219. Telephone: 513-684-3262. Web site: http://www.nps.gov/wiho/index.htm

Woodrow Wilson

Woodrow Wilson was sworn into office as president in 1913 and served two terms. After leading the nation through World War I, he worked for peace and helped set up the League of Nations, an organization where countries could solve their disputes peacefully. Many believe this was Wilson's finest accomplishment.

1,400 Love Letters

Born in Staunton, Virginia, just before the Civil War, in 1856, young Thomas Woodrow Wilson had two sisters and a brother. Tommie liked playing baseball, riding horseback, and playing chess, but he disliked school. He didn't learn to read until he was nearly eleven years old. His teachers described him as "bright enough but not interested."

As a young man, Woodrow (who had dropped his first name) felt that he was ugly. When he proposed marriage to his first love and she refused him, he believed it was because he was unattractive.

Wilson entered Davidson College at the age of sixteen, but he suffered a physical breakdown and returned home. He later went to the College of New Jersey (now Princeton University) and enrolled at the University of Virginia Law School, but again he developed health problems and returned home. He continued his studies at home and earned a law degree, but he soon decided that law was not for him.

He switched to the study of political history and entered Johns Hopkins University, where he thrived. There he wrote his first book on government and received a Ph.D. in political science, our only president to earn a doctoral degree.

Finally, things were working out for him. He met Ellen Axson, the oldest daughter of a prominent Presbyterian minister, at church one morning. Woodrow is supposed to have remarked, "What a bright pretty face! What splendid laughing eyes!" A few months later, he proposed marriage, although he was afraid she would refuse him. She did not and they lived happily until her death in the White House at the age of fifty-four. It is said that the Wilsons exchanged some 1,400 love letters!

Women Won the Right to Vote

Woodrow Wilson had grown into a tall, striking figure who radiated power and presence. Historians have said that his flashing eyes held a "splendid intelligence." The ugly duckling had turned into a swan.

After a decade as a professor, writer, and lecturer, Wilson was chosen as president of Princeton University and served from 1902 to 1910. During his time at Princeton, he became well-known in New Jersey politics and was later elected governor. From there he went on to become our twenty-eighth president.

During Wilson's administration, women won the right to vote, and Prohibition, which forbade the making, sale, and shipment of alcoholic beverages, was enacted. Wilson also did his best to keep the United States out of World War I, but by 1917, the United States was swept into fighting against Germany, Austria-Hungary, and Turkey. After the

Wilson Firsts

The first White House press conference was held by Woodrow Wilson on March 15, 1913, soon after he was elected. About 125 newspeople attended the event.

Wilson was also the first president to appoint a woman. Her name was Annette Adams Abbot and she served as assistant attorney general for a little over a year.

United States and the Allies—including Great Britain, France, Italy, and Russia—had won the war in 1918, Wilson urged all the countries to join the League of Nations, but Congress refused to allow the United States to join the League. Wilson's efforts were appreciated in other parts of the world, however, and he was awarded the Nobel Peace Prize in 1920.

While President Wilson was busy with peace programs and presidential duties, Ellen was not idle. She was distressed at the terrible living conditions of people who resided in the tumbledown shacks in the alleys near the White House. Thanks to her concern, Congress passed the Ellen Wilson Bill, which provided for tearing down the squalid buildings and constructing better housing for the inhabitants. Ellen also established the first rest rooms for women workers in government offices!

She had studied art briefly in New York City and still painted. Ellen had a studio with a skylight installed at the White House and found time for painting despite her official duties. She also planned beautiful weddings for two of the Wilsons' three daughters, who were married within six months of each other.

How to Shake Hands

Like other presidents, Wilson had to shake hands with so many people at public functions that his hand sometimes became sore. That is, until he invented his own method of shaking hands. He would put his middle finger down and join the index and ring fingers above it. In that way, people could not get a grip and his hand would slide through theirs!

"The Secret President"

Ellen died in 1914. Then, through mutual friends, Wilson met Edith Galt, a pretty forty-three-year-old widow. They were both lonely and liked each other right away. After their first meeting, the president began courting Edith, taking her for walks, automobile rides, and trips on the presidential yacht. Their mutual admiration turned to love, and they were married in 1915 in a quiet ceremony in the bride's Washington, D.C., home.

As Wilson guided the nation through World War I, Edith got out her sewing machine and made clothes for the troops. She joined the Red Cross and served coffee and sandwiches at soldiers' canteens in Washington, D.C. She also bought sheep to keep the White House lawn trim and tidy. (The leader of the flock, a ram called "Old Ike," was rumored to chew tobacco.) The sheep's wool was sold at an auction to benefit the Red Cross.

After the war, President Wilson, exhausted from touring the country trying to get support for the League of Nations, collapsed and suffered a stroke. Edith took over many of the routine duties and details of government. During this time she was often called "the secret president" and "the first woman to run the government," although she did not try to initiate programs.

After his last term in 1921, the disabled Wilson retired, broken in health and spirit. He and Edith moved to an attractive four-story red-brick townhouse with an elevator, on S Street in Washington, D.C. There, the former president lived in seclusion until his death in 1924. He is buried at the National Cathedral in Washington, D.C. Edith lived until 1961, a respected figure in capital society.

Wilson once said, "Ideas live, men die." He was right, for today the idea of the League of Nations lives on in the United Nations.

☆ Visit the ☆ Woodrow Wilson House

The house in which Woodrow Wilson spent his last days contains the furniture, trophies, souvenirs, and keepsakes of Wilson's lifetime. These belongings are exactly as they were when he lived there and offer a special look into the private life of the man. The house is also a National Historic Landmark and sits in the heart of Embassy Row, an exclusive area close to downtown Washington, D.C. It is the only presidential museum in the nation's capital.

Although the books in the former president's original library were donated to the Library of Congress, the museum holds a collection about Wilson and his presidency, and his archives contain a rich collection of photographs and selected papers.

The Woodrow Wilson House is in Washington, D.C. Open Tuesday through Sunday, except New Year's Day, Thanksgiving, and Christmas, 10 A.M. to 4 P.M. Adults $4. Student discounts. For more information: Woodrow Wilson House, 2340 S Street NW, Washington, DC 20008. Telephone: 202-387-4062. Web site: http://www.nthp.org/main/sites/wilsonhouse.htm

Warren Gamaliel Harding

Never had an administration been so bogged down in scandals as was Harding's. Although he tried to solve some of the problems resulting from World War I, he was not a hardworking leader, and many of the people he appointed to important positions were crooked. This man who loved people and hoped to become the most beloved U.S. president was ruined by bad judgment.

He Loved the Smell of Ink

Warren Harding, the twenty-ninth president of the United States, was born in Corsica (now Blooming Grove), Ohio, on November 2, 1865. The son of a country doctor, he was such a beautiful baby that people said he looked like a girl. Although his parents had seven other children, Warren was his mother's favorite.

He was a good student, and an outstanding speaker, but he was not a leader. Warren seemed happiest when he was just one of the gang. He especially liked to ride along in the horse-drawn buggy when his father visited patients.

Dr. Harding bought the local newspaper business when Warren was ten years old. The boy went to work as a printer's apprentice, known as a "printer's devil." From day one, he loved the smell of ink and the clatter of the presses and spent every moment he could spare from school in the newspaper office.

When he was fourteen, Warren started college. He didn't study much, but he made lots of friends, joined the debate society, and started the school newspaper. The paper was four pages long and included advertising, local news, jokes, and a column that Warren wrote.

After he graduated, he returned home and took a job as a teacher in a country school. A year later he began selling insurance, but he made so many math mistakes that he quit. The only career that really interested him was newspaper work, so he got a job on the Marion, Ohio, *Mirror.* There he did everything: selling advertising space, reporting, setting type, and running errands for the owner. The job didn't last long, however, for Warren spent too much time away from the job, talking politics with friends.

Although he had been fired from the *Mirror,* he still loved newspaper work, so he and three friends bought a small paper called the *Star.* Harding had finally found his occupation as a newspaper owner and the paper was successful.

Harding was a strikingly good-looking young man with a gift for making and keeping friends. He knew everyone in Marion and was one of the most sought-after young bachelors in the area. One of the women who pursued him was Florence Kling DeWolfe, a divorced woman of thirty-one and the daughter of the richest man in town. Since "The Duchess," as Harding called her, was not especially attractive, people were amazed when the handsome twenty-six-year-old and Florence were married.

Florence started running the newspaper to give her husband time to concentrate on politics. Legend says that she was a tough businesswoman who even spanked the newsboys when they did not make their deliveries on time. People later said that her drive and determination helped put her husband in the presidency. She often said, "I have only one real hobby—my husband." Although the Hardings had no children, they had a dog named Laddie Boy. Both were crazy about the rambunctious Airedale and were often photographed playing with him.

His Attendance Record Was Terrible

In 1899, Harding was elected to the Ohio state senate where he served two terms. Following that, he was lieutenant governor of Ohio, chairman of the Republican convention, and then a U.S. senator.

Harding's record as a senator was unremarkable and his attendance record was terrible. Whenever a controversial bill was to be voted on, the eager-to-please Harding did not appear. When he did show up, he voted as he was told to by his party. Never one to make enemies, he spent much of his time playing golf with influential people and being helpful to party leaders. In 1921, he became the "dark horse" candidate for the presidency, with Calvin Coolidge as his running mate.

The Worst Collection of Scandals

Harding was inaugurated our twenty-ninth president in 1921 with an enthusiastic Duchess at his side. He was the first president to ride to his inauguration in an automobile. Since he had little political experience, he appointed a cabinet and then let them make most decisions. This proved to be a great mistake, for several of his appointees turned out to be crooked.

Florence Harding has been called a "folksy" kind of First Lady. She tried to mingle with people every chance she got. She often came downstairs when White House tours were being conducted and showed the crowd the sights. Florence also took special pleasure in taking flowers from the White House gardens to World War I veterans in Walter Reed Army Hospital. She considered her most successful entertainment a big veterans' garden party on the White House lawn. Florence had bought a new hat for the occasion but decided to wear the one she usually wore to Walter Reed, so "the boys" would recognize her.

In 1923, President Harding left on a trip to tour Alaska (the first president to visit that territory). Traveling with him was Secretary of Commerce Herbert Hoover, who later reported that Harding seemed jumpy and depressed. At one point, Harding asked Hoover what he would

More About Laddie Boy

Laddie Boy sometimes attended cabinet meetings with Harding, where he sat on his own hand-carved chair. He had his own servant, and reporters sometimes "quoted" Laddie Boy in mock interviews. On his birthday, all the neighborhood dogs were invited to the White House for a party!

do if he were president and learned of misconduct in his administration. Hoover replied that he would make it public. After the two men talked, Harding was very pale and walked the decks of the ship the rest of the night.

Returning from Alaska, Harding suffered a massive heart attack in San Francisco and died. Following his death, the nation's grief soon turned to shock. Scandals came to light involving members of Harding's cabinet who had taken bribes, and other officials were accused of stealing government funds. Both Harding's reputation and the nation were severely damaged by the worst collection of scandals yet seen in the country.

☆ Visit ☆ President Harding's Home

President Harding's home in Marion, Ohio, is open to the public. The large Victorian house with sparkling white trim has both upstairs and downstairs porches where the Hardings and their friends and neighbors spent much time.

Harding also built a small cottage behind the main house as headquarters for the National Press Corp. "The press building," as it was called, is now a museum that houses many interesting artifacts of Harding's private life.

President Harding's Home is in Marion, Ohio. Open daily Memorial Day through Labor Day, Wednesday through Saturday, 9:30 A.M. to 5 P.M., Sunday noon to 5 P.M. Open by appointment only April, May, September, and October. Adults $2.50. Student discounts. For more information: President Harding's Home, 380 Mount Vernon Avenue, Marion, OH 43302. Telephone: 740-387-9630. Web site: http://www.ohiohistory.org/places/harding/index.html

Calvin Coolidge

Historians say that President Calvin Coolidge was more distinguished for his character than for his achievements. He assumed office after scandals had rocked the Harding administration. Although Coolidge had been vice president under Warren Harding, he had had nothing to do with the misconduct, and he was determined to clean up the office of the president.

Wearing Only His White Long Underwear

John Calvin Coolidge was born in Plymouth Notch, Vermont, on July 4, 1872. He had a younger sister, Abigail Grace. His family, who'd lived in the small village for generations, believed in love of God and family, hard work, and public service. His grandfather and father had both served as state legislators. His father was also a prosperous farmer and storekeeper. His mother, a quiet woman, died when Calvin was twelve. "The greatest grief that can come to a boy came to me," he later said about his mother's death.

Calvin adored his grandfather, who raised Arabian horses and kept peacocks. The boy had his own horse, and he would even ride standing on the horse's back. Calvin also liked to ice skate, play baseball, and fish.

Calvin and his sister attended a one-room schoolhouse. Calvin was very quiet in the classroom and rarely spoke up unless he had something important to say. When he started high school, he went to Black River Academy twelve miles away.

Cal entered Amherst College and graduated in 1895. He began studying law that year and joined a law firm in Northampton, Massachusetts, in 1897. One morning Calvin was shaving in front of a mirror in his bedroom wearing only his white long underwear and for some reason, a hat. He was startled to hear giggling and looked up to see a pretty girl standing on the sidewalk. She had gotten a glimpse of him through the window and was bent over in helpless laughter. Coolidge was horribly embarrassed, but he smiled at her before pulling the shade over the window. He didn't know it, but he'd just met his future wife, Grace Goodhue!

The lively, outgoing Grace taught at Clark Institute for the Deaf across the street from Coolidge's boardinghouse. Not long after this strange "non-meeting," he was introduced to her at a social gathering. They began to date and soon fell in love. Since he was a man of few words, Calvin proposed by baldly declaring, "I am going to be married to you." Although it wasn't romantic, Grace knew her man, knew that he loved her, and accepted.

The Coolidges had two sons, though only one lived to adulthood. As Calvin rose higher in public office and grew busier, it was often Grace who played baseball and fished with the boys. She had always loved the outdoors and tried to ignore her mother's advice to learn to make bread! Grace, who also had a good sense of humor, confessed to a college friend, "I have always turned pale at the mention of a cake of yeast."

He Was Now the President

To promote his law practice, Coolidge ran for local public office. He found that, shy as he was, he enjoyed politics and had a talent for it. Eventually he was elected to the state legislature and then became the mayor of Northampton, Massachusetts. In 1918 he was elected governor of Massachusetts. While in office, he settled a strike of the Boston police. He was the first to tell officers, "There is no right to strike against the public safety by anybody, anywhere, anytime." This action gained him national attention and he was chosen to run as vice president with Warren Harding.

One night, while visiting his father on the farm near Plymouth Notch, Vice President Coolidge was awakened after midnight by a loud pounding at the door. His secretary, his chauffeur, and a reporter had come to announce that President Harding was dead from a heart attack and that Coolidge was now the president.

By 2:30 A.M. reporters were swarming around the house. Everyone thought Coolidge would rush back to Washington and be sworn in by a member of the Supreme Court, but that wasn't the new president's style. By the flickering light of a kerosene lamp, he was given the oath of office as the nation's thirtieth president by his father, who was a notary and a justice of the peace.

When the ceremony was over, the new chief executive said good-bye to the hastily assembled witnesses, blew out the lamp, and went back to bed. Coolidge headed for the White House the next day, but only after a visit to the graves of his mother and grandfather in a nearby cemetery.

Personal Honesty, Strong Moral Values

The greatest problem the new chief executive faced was the mess left by the preceding administration. Coolidge had a little more than a year of Harding's term to serve, but he set to work cleaning up the scandals and extravagances of the Harding administration and reducing the national debt. He was reelected in 1924 and served until 1928. Coolidge is probably best remembered for his personal honesty, strong moral values, thrift, and modesty.

After Coolidge was elected president, many people said that Grace became the most popular person in Washington. Her zest for life, friendly ways, and unaffected manner charmed everyone. She also loved stylish clothes, which set off her good looks. (Friends said that Coolidge's one indulgence was to buy Grace beautiful things.) But for his part, Silent Cal enjoyed such simple pleasures as sitting on the front porch after dinner and watching the people pass by on Pennsylvania Avenue. So many people stopped to stare at him, however, that he had to give up this simple way of relaxing.

The Coolidge family had one of the largest collections of pets in the White House, including several cats, canaries and many other birds, a goose, a wallaby, a donkey, a lion cub, and twelve dogs. Grace especially loved her collie, Rob Roy. Someone once sent a live raccoon to be cooked and served for

Silent Cal

Some people said that "Silent Cal," as he was often called, looked sour enough to have been weaned on a pickle. He was not grouchy, but he was a man of few words. And he did have a sense of humor. Once a young woman sitting next to Coolidge at a dinner party confided that she had made a bet that she could get more than two words of conversation from him. His reply was, "You lose."

the Coolidges' Thanksgiving dinner. The whole family was horrified, especially Grace. She named the little animal Rebecca and kept her as a pet.

Although the Republican party urged Coolidge to run in 1928, he declined. The death of one of his two sons during the 1924 campaign had nearly broken Coolidge's heart and he no longer had any interest in politics. The fourteen-year-old Calvin junior had developed a blister from playing tennis in sneakers without socks. The blister became infected, and the boy died of blood poisoning four days later. Coolidge wrote a friend, "The power and the glory of the presidency went with him."

☆ Visit ☆ PLYMOUTH NOTCH

Today, the entire village of Plymouth Notch, where Calvin Coolidge grew up, is a part of the National Register of Historic Places. The community of colorful clapboard houses is almost unchanged since the early twentieth century. Coolidge's homestead, the homes of his friends and neighbors, the community church, the cheese factory, the one-room schoolhouse, and the general store have been carefully preserved and contain most of their original furnishings.

There are fourteen places to visit in Plymouth Notch, including the cemetery where six generations of Coolidges are buried. It is a serene spot, surrounded by mountains and shady old trees. In keeping with the president's lack of pretense, his gravestone is a simply marked marble stone.

The Plymouth Notch Historic District is in the village of Plymouth Notch, Vermont, approximately 20 miles east of Rutland. Open daily, late May through mid-October, 9:30 A.M. to 5:30 P.M. Adults $4, children under 14 free. For more information: Plymouth Notch Historic District, P.O. Box 247, Plymouth Notch, VT 05056. Telephone: 802-672-3773. Web site: http://www.calvin-coolidge.org

Herbert Clark Hoover

Herbert Hoover was the first president born west of the Mississippi and the first to enter the White House as a multimillionaire. Seven months after he took office, the stock market crashed, beginning the Great Depression. He left office in 1933 an unpopular man because of the nation's dissatisfaction with the way he handled the hard times. But he died, years later, one of the nation's most respected former presidents because of his service to victims of World War II.

His Favorite Teacher Wanted to Adopt Him

Born in the village of West Branch, Iowa, in 1874, Herbert was the son of a blacksmith. He and his older brother and younger sister grew up in a peaceful Quaker household.

His father died of pneumonia when the boy was six years old and his mother took in sewing to keep the family together. Herbert was a big help to her. He gathered wood for the cookstove, fed the chickens, and helped care for his little sister. Still, there was time to play, and he and his friends dammed the creek and made a swimming hole. In the winter, they whizzed down the snowy hills on their sleds.

When Herbert was ten years old, his mother contracted typhoid fever and died. His favorite teacher wanted to adopt him, but Herbert's relatives felt it was not seemly because she was not married. Instead, the boy was sent to live with his uncle, a country doctor in Oregon.

Although his uncle was a stern man and lectured Herbert constantly on making something of himself, the two did have some good times together. Sometimes the doctor asked the boy to ride along when he went to visit patients. During these rides, his uncle told exciting stories of Civil War battles and his experiences helping runaway slaves reach Canada.

Herbert had a good life in the Northwest, although he missed his brother and sister. He was often bored and restless in school, yet he made good grades. After high school, he worked his way through Stanford University, where he took an engineering degree with the first graduating class of 1895.

While a student at Stanford, Hoover met his future wife, Lou Henry, who was the first woman to major in geology there. Herbert, a senior, was in charge of a Saturday freshman geology field trip when he noticed Lou. That day the attractive girl with black hair and blue eyes wore a hiking skirt, a soft leather hat, and boots. Hoover later said that the outfit made her look "very fetching." From that day on, neither of them missed one of the outdoor classes. Soon they began to date and the tall pair was often seen walking hand in hand on the Stanford campus.

Herbert proposed marriage to Lou in a cablegram from Australia, where he had gone as a mining engineer. The wedding was planned around the young couple's departure by ship for China where Hoover was to work. Following the wedding, the couple each went home to change. As they boarded the ship, the pair was amazed to see they were dressed in nearly identical new brown traveling suits, which neither knew that the other had purchased.

Lou—and later their two sons, Herbert junior and Allan—traveled the world with Hoover, living in countries that were often dangerous and undeveloped. Some of these places were Australia, New Zealand, Japan, China, Burma, Ceylon, Egypt, and Russia. By the time Herbert Hoover, Jr., was a year old, he had been around the world twice. The Hoovers were all outdoor people and were happiest when they were knee-deep in some mountain stream fishing for trout or hiking in the hills.

One of the Ten Greatest Living Americans

When the United States entered World War I on April 6, 1917, the Hoovers were living in London. The U.S. ambassador asked Hoover to help 120,000 stranded Americans get back to the United States. Hoover did such a good job that President Wilson appointed him director of the new U.S. Food Administration. He distributed food and supplies throughout Europe during the war.

During this time, a *New York Times* poll named Hoover one of the ten greatest living Americans. In 1921, he was appointed secretary of commerce and served under both Harding and Coolidge. Later, when Coolidge refused to run for reelection, the Republican party nominated Hoover as its presidential candidate. He won and began his unsuccessful attempt to lead the country through the Depression.

The Hoovers moved into the White House in 1929, where Lou welcomed visitors with poise and dignity. She paid, with her own money, for reproductions of James Monroe's furniture for a historic sitting room and restored Lincoln's study for her husband's use. The Hoovers brought many travel mementos with them, including South American rugs, Oriental art, exotic birds in cages, and books in many languages. They entertained lavishly, using their own private funds for social events.

In 1932, Hoover was defeated by Franklin D. Roosevelt. After leaving the White House, Hoover continued his public service and gained the respect of the world for his humanitarian efforts. Of the U.S. presidents, only Theodore Roosevelt had more book titles to his credit than Herbert Hoover. He also gave lectures and continued to be active in public service until his death in 1964.

First Lady, or First Girl Scout?

Mrs. Hoover was especially interested in the Girl Scouts of America, which had been established in 1912. The organization offered her a chance to lead young girls in the outdoors and to teach them to love the natural world. Through the years she served as everything from troop leader to president of the Girl Scouts. She said that because of the way she lived, she had been a scout all her life, even before the group existed.

☆ Visit the ☆ HERBERT HOOVER Presidential Library and Museum

The Herbert Hoover Presidential Library and Museum is one of nine presidential libraries administered by the National Archives and Record Administration. The facility, opened on Hoover's eighty-eighth birthday on August 10, 1962, was extensively renovated and expanded in 1992. Tours begin in the rotunda where a 16-foot red granite map of the world is emblazoned with fifty-seven brass sheaves of wheat—one for each country where Hoover provided food relief. Mounted on the wall nearby are glass-etched portraits of Hoover that stand 8 feet tall.

Galleries off the rotunda feature lifelike figures of Hoover at different stages of his life. Other interesting displays depict the Hoovers' life in China and a recreation of Suite 31-A in the Waldorf Astoria Towers, in New York City, the Hoovers' home after his leaving the presidency.

The Hoover Presidential Library and Museum is located in West Branch, Iowa. Open daily, except New Year's Day, Thanksgiving, and Christmas, 9 A.M. to 5 P.M. Adults $2, children under 16 free. For more information: Hoover National Historic Site, West Branch, IA 52358. Telephone: 319-643-2541. Web site: http://www.hoover.nara.gov/

Franklin Delano Roosevelt

Franklin D. Roosevelt took office on March 4, 1933, the fourth year of the Great Depression. The country was on the verge of disaster. He took immediate control during his first 100 days of office. FDR, as he was commonly known, not only pulled the country out of its deadly slump with his decisive policies, he also led the nation through World War II.

"Consider Yourself Spanked"

Our thirty-second president was born on January 30, 1882, in Hyde Park, New York, the child of wealthy parents. His half brother, James, was already an adult, and his father, a former financier, had retired to his country estate by the time Franklin was born. The older Roosevelt raised champion trotting horses and lived the life of a country gentleman.

Franklin and his father, whom the boy called "Popsy," were very close. One day Franklin played a mean trick on his governess. His mother felt that the little boy should be punished and told his father. Mr. Roosevelt solemnly called his son into his study. As Franklin stood before him, his father sternly said, "Consider yourself spanked."

Hyde Park was a wonderful place to grow up. Franklin had his own pony, named Debbie, and acres of land to explore. In the summer he swam, played tennis, and canoed on the Hudson River or sailed at the Roosevelts' summer home on Campobello Island off the Maine coast. In the winter he skated, iceboated, and tobogganed.

Although he loved sports and the outdoors, Franklin enjoyed reading and collecting stamps as well. Mark Twain was his favorite writer, but he also read anything he could find concerning the U.S. Navy.

Franklin was tutored at home until he was fourteen. By that age he had traveled to Europe eight times and he seems to have had some adventurous times. On one bicycle tour, he and his pals were arrested for four different crimes: knocking over a goose with a bicycle, picking cherries from a branch hanging over the road, entering a walled city after sundown, and wheeling their bikes into a railroad station!

Franklin attended private schools, where he was an average student. By the time he was seventeen, he was over 6 feet tall and strikingly handsome. He hoped to attend the U.S. Naval Academy, but his father, who had gone to Harvard, insisted that his son do the same. While he was at Harvard, his cousin, Theodore Roosevelt, was elected president. Teddy had always been different from his relatives, most of whom considered politics "tacky." Franklin was greatly influenced by Teddy and decided that he, too, must go into politics to build a better world, so he went to law school. At this time, another cousin became important in his life: Anna Eleanor Roosevelt, actually a fifth cousin, once removed.

Eleanor's Childhood

Eleanor's early years were painful. Her mother, a beautiful woman, was cold and distant to her child, even calling the little girl "Granny" because she was so serious. Eleanor's mother died when she was eight and her father when she was ten. Eleanor went to live with her grandmother Hall, a stern and disapproving woman. Eleanor later said that as a child she was always afraid of being scolded and was sure that nobody liked her.

A Scrappy Fighter

Franklin's mother, Sara Roosevelt, a very domineering woman, didn't think the timid Eleanor was good enough for her son. But although she did everything possible to break up the pair, Sara was unsuccessful. They were soon engaged to be married and Teddy, cousin to both Franklin and Eleanor, gave away the bride.

In 1910, Franklin was elected to the New York legislature at only twenty-eight years of age. Many people were ready to write him off as a "rich kid" who was just playing at politics, but he surprised everyone by becoming a hardworking senator and a scrappy fighter for better government. Following two terms, he was chosen assistant secretary of the navy under President Woodrow Wilson.

Then in 1921, Franklin, Eleanor, and their five children took a vacation at Campobello. The family was having a wonderful time until Roosevelt awakened one morning with terrible pains in his back and legs. He had been stricken with polio, a debilitating and sometimes fatal disease. The doctors said he would be crippled if he even survived.

Roosevelt struggled for life. He slowly got better, but his legs were paralyzed. He would never again stand without the aid of braces or crutches, but he would not give in to the disease. He learned to get about using heavy leg braces, crutches, or a wheelchair. Although he would never run and play with his children again, he never gave in to self-pity and even made jokes about his condition. Often when he was ready to leave or move on, he would say, "Well, gotta run."

He reentered politics, and by 1928, he was governor of New York. Then came the Great Depression. Businesses failed, banks closed, people lost their jobs and stood in bread lines for food. President Hoover didn't seem to do anything to better the terrible conditions, so Americans were looking for a strong new leader.

"This Great Nation Will Survive"

Roosevelt swept into office with a stunning majority in the election of 1932. He immediately set to work to restore hope to the nation. He

Famous Fala

Probably the president's closest companion was Fala, his Scottish terrier. Fala followed Roosevelt everywhere or rode like a little king on his lap in the wheelchair. When Roosevelt was on an official visit to the USS *Baltimore*, sailors eager for a presidential souvenir plucked out so many of the little dog's hairs that he was left nearly bald. Roosevelt was furious when he saw the scraggly Fala. He continued to take the little dog along on his travels, but when the Scottie was away from his master, aides made sure that nobody snipped off any of his dark coat.

told the country in his inaugural address, "This great nation will survive. The only thing we have to fear is fear itself." He also regularly addressed the nation in radio "fireside chats," reassuring Americans that he would help them.

Roosevelt tackled the Great Depression like a warrior. His plan of action, called the New Deal, included dozens of programs to pull the country through its economic crisis and put people back to work. FDR served for four terms, from 1932 to his death in 1945. No other president had ever served so long or ever will again, since two terms are now the limit.

The Roosevelts' four sons and one daughter were nearly adults when their father became president. Eleanor, the former timid young bride who was very independent by now, feared the move to the White House would make her "a prisoner in a gilded cage." Instead, she grew into one of the strongest and most respected First Ladies who ever lived. She held weekly press conferences, lectured throughout the country, wrote a daily newspaper column, and had her own radio program. She traveled the world, acting as the eyes and ears of her disabled husband. In fact, Eleanor traveled so much, the Secret Service gave her the code name of "Rover."

After the Depression, Roosevelt had to face World War II. He knew that the United States must enter the war or the Allies would be defeated and democracy destroyed around the world. It was a long and bitter struggle, but the Axis powers were finally defeated.

In 1945, Roosevelt attended a conference with Winston Churchill, the prime minister of Great Britain, and Joseph Stalin, the leader of the Soviet Union (Russia), to settle terms of the peace. Following the long trip home, a tired and haggard Roosevelt retreated to his cottage at Warm Springs, Georgia, often called the Little White House.

One day while there, he suddenly put his hand to his head and complained of a terrible headache. He slumped down in his chair. One of the staff called a doctor, but the president died on April 12, 1945, of a cerebral hemorrhage.

After her husband's death, Eleanor went on to serve the public for seventeen more years.

CAMP DAVID

President Roosevelt, wanting to escape the summer heat of Washington, D.C., established a retreat in the wooded Catoctin mountains in Maryland. He named the place Shangri-La after the fabled kingdom in James Hilton's book *Lost Horizon*. Later, President Eisenhower renamed the retreat after his grandson, David.

The buildings are rustic, but the facility is like a private resort, with a golf putting green, swimming pool, movie theater, bowling alley, and beautiful hiking trails and bridle paths. Government business is also conducted at Camp David. Many international conferences and negotiations have been held there.

She was appointed as a delegate to the United Nations and was chairman of the Commission on Human Rights. She presided over her large family at her cottage at Hyde Park and led a busy social life until her death in 1962.

☆ Visit the ☆ FRANKLIN D. ROOSEVELT Home and Library

The Franklin D. Roosevelt Library was the first presidential library. It lies in the peaceful countryside, about a two-hour drive from New York City. Built of Dutchess County fieldstone, the building includes many exhibits that offer an intimate glimpse into the life of the Roosevelt family. Both Franklin and Eleanor are buried in the rose garden.

A very popular exhibit is FDR's automobile. The jazzy Ford Phaeton is equipped with special hand controls. Many photographs show a jaunty FDR sailing along a Georgia country road in the convertible with the top down, his hat brim turned up, and Fala riding shotgun in the passenger seat.

The Victorian mansion at Hyde Park where Franklin Roosevelt was born is also open to the public. One of its most attractive features is one that Roosevelt loved, a screened porch that overlooks the rolling lawns with a dramatic view of the Hudson Valley.

The Franklin D. Roosevelt Home and Library is at Hyde Park, New York. Open daily, except New Year's Day, Thanksgiving, and Christmas, 9 A.M. to 5 P.M. Adults $4, children under 16 free. For more information: Roosevelt Library, 529 Albany Post Road, Hyde Park, NY 12538. Telephone: 914-229-8114. Web site: http://www.academic.marist.edu/fdr/

Harry S. Truman

Harry Truman had been the reluctant vice president of the United States for only eighty-three days when FDR died on April 12, 1945. The little-known midwestern politician completed Roosevelt's term and was reelected. This thirty-third president brought World War II to an end and led the country through difficult times with courage and determination, even though he said that being president was like "having a tiger at one's tail every hour of the day."

A Gift for Leadership

Harry was born to hardworking parents in Lamar, Missouri, in 1884, one of three children. Harry's middle initial, "S," was not an abbreviation; his mother and father simply could not decide whether the baby's middle name should be Shippe, after his father's father, or Solomon, after his mother's father.

Harry spent his childhood in Independence, Missouri. Although he did well in school, his thick glasses made it difficult for him to play sports. He was good-natured and well-liked, but he was often lonely and spent many hours at the Independence Public Library. With his mother's encouragement, he became a good piano player and he continued to enjoy playing for the rest of his life.

His father was active in politics and often took young Harry with him to conventions, where the boy was excited by the cheering and the fiery speeches. When election day rolled around, his parents had a hard time explaining to an angry Harry that he couldn't vote!

Harry's secret dream was to attend the U.S. Military Academy at West Point, but he knew his poor eyesight made that impossible. As it turned out, he did not even get to attend college. His father made some bad investments, which wiped out the family savings.

His parents moved to the farm of Mrs. Truman's father. Harry stayed in Independence and held a series of jobs—as a bank clerk, theater usher, and piano player. A few years later his father, unable to manage the farm alone, called Harry home to help.

The young man farmed for eleven years. The hard physical work built up his strength, and he became more sure of himself. Evenings, he often went to Democratic party meetings. He also served on the school board and joined the National Guard. During this time, Harry found he had a gift for leadership.

When World War I came, Harry was commissioned as a field artillery officer. He took part in some of the worst battles in France, including action in the Vosges Mountains and in the Argonne Forest. His troops trusted him and he proved his courage time and again.

Following the war, Harry returned to Missouri to marry Bess Wallace, whom he had adored since he was in high school. Bess was one of the most popular girls in Independence. She loved to go to parties, play cards, and dance. She was good at sports, too, especially baseball, tennis, and basketball. She also held strong opinions and was not afraid to express them. Bess's mother was less than thrilled about the marriage. She thought her daughter could have done better than a farmer's son who didn't even have a college education. (In fact, Mrs. Wallace never really considered Harry a success, even after he became president!)

Elected to the U.S. Senate in 1934, Truman quickly became a popular and effective lawmaker. He was a strong supporter of President Roosevelt, and when FDR ran for a fourth term, Truman was chosen as his running mate.

"He Done His Damndest"

Following Roosevelt's death, Harry Truman became president. He faced difficult decisions during these years, including whether to use the atomic bomb to end the war with Japan. People still debate whether his decision to drop the bomb was correct, but there is no question that he thought long and hard about it.

During the time the Trumans were in the White House, Bess tried to stay out of the public eye, although Harry loved to tease her by introducing her to everybody as "the boss." She did not enjoy politics and disliked "life in a goldfish bowl," as she described the lack of privacy in the White House. But she made an effort to be with Harry on campaign trips and tours across the country. Bess fulfilled her social obligations as First Lady, but she did no more than was necessary. As her husband said, "she was not especially interested in the formalities and pomp that inevitably surround the family of the president."

The Trumans' only daughter, Margaret, was twenty-one when her father became president. Although she, too, tried to keep her life private, reporters tried to follow her on dates and outings with her friends. Margaret was a sensible girl, however, and handled the situation graciously. She also had an especially supportive relationship with her parents. Like the Three Musketeers, the three Trumans stuck together come what might!

Truman often worked to the point of exhaustion while he was president. He was happy to return to Missouri after his terms were finished. Some 10,000 people waited at the train station for Harry, Bess, and

Food Fight!

One night at the White House, when the Trumans had watermelon for dessert, Harry playfully flipped one of the seeds off his thumb toward Bess. She quickly fired one back. Margaret joined the free-for-all, and soon a watermelon-seed fight was raging. When the butler, unaware of the battle, came in to remove the plates, he saw what was happening and started laughing at the sight of the seeds ricocheting round the dining room. He didn't take any chances, though; he took shelter out of the line of fire until the fight ended.

Proud Papa

Margaret Truman had a pleasant singing voice and studied music for years. In 1950, she gave a concert at Constitution Hall. When Truman read the *Washington Post* the next morning, he found that the music critic had given Margaret's concert a terrible review. Truman was so angry that he wrote the paper a letter of protest. In an effort to embarrass the president, the music critic published Truman's letter in the paper. Truman was not in the least embarrassed. He said, "I did not write the letter as the president, I wrote it as a human being." A poll revealed that over 80 percent of the American people agreed with what Truman had done as a father.

Margaret when they arrived back in Independence. Another 5,000 lined the neighborhood streets around their house. Local people had known the Trumans for years and treated them as "just hometown folks."

Harry Truman died in a Kansas City hospital on December 25, 1972. In an interview in 1950, he remarked, "The best epitaph I ever saw was on Boot Hill in Tombstone, Arizona. It said 'Here Lies Jack Williams. He Done His Damndest.'" History tells us that Harry Truman also did his damndest!

Visit INDEPENDENCE and the HARRY S. TRUMAN National Historic Site

Today, the Trumans' gracious old house and much of the town of Independence are the Harry S. Truman National Historic Site. The Truman Library and Museum was the pride of Truman's retirement. He spent many hours in its planning and often worked there six and a half days a week after it was finished. Always an early riser, the elderly former president often got there before any of the staff and started answering the telephone, much to the astonishment of callers.

In the museum gallery are various cars belonging to the Trumans, including an elegant 1950 Lincoln Cosmopolitan from the White House fleet. The 20-foot-long limousine has a red, white, and blue license plate with stars and stripes reading "Inaugural I."

The Truman Library and Museum is 10 miles east of Kansas City, Missouri, at U.S. Highway 24 and Delaware in Independence, Missouri. Open daily, except New Year's Day, Thanksgiving, and Christmas, 9 A.M. to 5 P.M. Adults $5, students under 15 free. For more information: Truman Library and Museum, 24 and Delaware, Independence, MO 64050. Telephone: 816-833-1400. Website: http://www.trumanlibrary.org/

The Truman Home at 219 North Delaware is open Tuesday through Saturday from the day after Memorial Day to the day before Labor Day, 9 A.M. to 5 P.M. Adults $2, students under 17 free. For more information: Harry S. Truman National Historic Site, 223 North Main Street, Independence, MO 64050. Telephone: 816-833-1400. Web site: http://www.nps.gov/hstr

Dwight David Eisenhower

Dwight David Eisenhower served as president from 1953 to 1961. He was a highly decorated five-star general who had not only been chief of staff of the U.S. Army but had commanded all Allied troops in Europe during World War II. Although he first served his country in the military, he later became known as a man of peace.

Ike Loved Adventure

Our thirty-fourth president was the third of seven sons born to poor but kind and peace-loving parents. Though he was born in Denison, Texas, on October 14, 1890, he grew up in Abilene, Kansas. He and his brothers received a strong religious training from their parents. The boys also learned to cook, wash dishes, and clean house. Although his mother hated nicknames, Dwight David soon became known as "Ike," a nickname he would carry for the rest of his life.

Even as a child, Ike loved adventure. Once, when the town of Abilene flooded, he and one of his brothers found a large board, big enough for the two of them to sit on. They hopped on the makeshift raft and floated all over town. They were having so much fun that they did not notice that they were about to be swept into a raging river. Although they were lucky that a neighbor saw what was about to happen and turned them back, they were not so lucky when they returned home. Their worried father met them at the door with a switch.

Ike was a good student, with a winning personality, and, like his brothers, he excelled in sports. In high school, he played both baseball and football, but football was his favorite and he made the varsity team.

Following high school graduation in 1911, Ike became a cadet at West Point. At the Point, Ike had a hard time learning to march and was put into the "Awkward Squad," until he could keep time properly. He was also a rebel and got a lot of demerits. He smoked cigarettes in front of his teachers and got demerits. He danced too wildly, more demerits. He was often late for class, more demerits. The punishment for getting too many demerits was extra marching. It is said that Ike was marching the whole time he was at West Point!

Still, he studied hard, although his first love was sports. When an injury ended his football playing, Ike was ready to drop out of school, but his classmates and instructors pleaded with him to stay. Ike went on to become the most famous member of his graduating class, which was known as "the class the stars fell on," because more than one-third of its members became generals.

During his first assignment in San Antonio, Texas, Ike met a peppy brunette named Mamie Doud, an eighteen-year-old with bangs and a great smile. They were married in 1916 and, as a military couple, traveled all over the world. Of their two sons, the elder died in childhood of scarlet fever, a tragedy Ike always spoke of as the greatest personal loss of his life. John, their younger son, would grow up to attend West Point and serve in Europe during the time his father was commander there.

Sportsman, Artist, Barbecue King

Eisenhower was an accomplished fly fisherman and a fine shot with both pistol and shotgun. He was a good golfer and played to win. Ike enjoyed his golf so much that the U.S. Golf Association built him a putting green near the White House so he could practice anytime he wanted to. He was also a good amateur painter and he liked to barbecue.

"Club Eisenhower"

Mamie quickly became what was considered to be the perfect army wife. She entertained with such lively parties that the Eisenhower apartment (and future homes) became known as "Club Eisenhower." Mamie could make a comfortable home anywhere Ike was posted.

Through the years, Eisenhower rose steadily through the ranks. In World War II, he was made commander of the U.S. forces in Europe. He planned and led the victorious June 6, 1944, D-Day invasion of Normandy, France, which hastened the end of the war. On December 10, 1944, Dwight David Eisenhower was promoted to the newly created rank of five-star general.

Ike returned from war a hero. As early as 1948, both the Democratic and Republican parties tried to get him to run for the presidency. Ike refused, for he basically disliked politics. Instead, he became president of Columbia University, then the supreme commander of the North Atlantic Treaty Organization (NATO) forces.

But in 1953, Eisenhower accepted the Republican party's nomination. "I like Ike" was the campaign slogan, and millions of Americans certainly did! He was elected by a landslide.

Calm and Prosperity

Eisenhower's term of office was a period of relative calm and prosperity in the United States. During his presidency, the Supreme Court desegregated schools in the United States. The National Aeronautics and Space Administration was established, and the first U.S. satellite, *Explorer I*, was launched. He improved the country's highways and created the Department of Health, Education and Welfare.

Ike was usually good-tempered with his staff, but his appointments secretary, Tom Stephens, noticed that the boss usually wore brown when he was grouchy. After that, Stephens would station himself at the window to watch Eisenhower walking toward the office. If he had on a brown suit, Stephens alerted the staff that the day looked "threatening."

Mamie Eisenhower thoroughly enjoyed her time as First Lady. Her warm personality made her one of the most entertaining hostesses in Washington. She gave lots of parties and dinners and also loved traveling about the country with Ike. She especially enjoyed sitting in the backseat of the presidential limousine and waving at the crowds.

Mamie Pink

Pink was Mamie's favorite color. One particular shade that she often wore became known as "Mamie pink." She also had another trademark: her hairstyle. She wore short bangs all her life. She started a trend when many women of her age began wearing their hair the same way.

After his last term in office, Ike and Mamie retired to their farm in Gettysburg, Pennsylvania. Following a fatal heart attack on March 28, 1969, Dwight David Eisenhower was laid to rest in the Place of Meditation in Eisenhower Center. Nearly ten years later Mamie was also interred there.

☆ Visit the ☆ EISENHOWER CENTER

When you visit Eisenhower Center in Abilene, Kansas, you'll find a complex of five buildings: the library, the visitors' center, the family home, the museum, and the Place of Meditation. The parklike grounds, covering several acres, look like a college campus. The area is watched over by an 11-foot statue of Eisenhower.

Most people first visit the family home, a modest dwelling whose tidy front parlor is still arranged as Ike's mother had it. Family photographs line the walls. With wooden rocking chairs, a big radio, potted plants, and a piano, this "best room" was usually off-limits to the six rambunctious Eisenhower boys.

The museum houses a gallery of life-size wax figures of famous World War II generals. Of special interest is the display of Eisenhower's uniforms, which includes the "Eisenhower jacket" that started a fashion trend.

The Eisenhower Library occupies a separate building and houses over 22 million documents. In addition to containing the papers of Eisenhower's time, the facility is known as one of the finest sources for the study of recent U.S. history and the presidency.

The Eisenhower Center is in Abilene, Kansas. Open daily, except New Year's Day, Thanksgiving, and Christmas, 9 A.M. to 4:45 P.M. Adults $1.50, children under 15 free. For more information: Eisenhower Center, Abilene, KS 67410. Telephone: 913-263-4751. Web site: http://www.eisenhower.utexas.edu

John Fitzgerald Kennedy

November 22, 1963. The motorcade of John Fitzgerald Kennedy wound slowly past cheering crowds in Dallas, Texas. In the open car, the handsome young president's hair ruffled in the breeze. His wife put a hand up to steady the small pink hat she wore. A heartbeat later, three rifle shots rang out in the clear Texas air and nothing would ever be the same. The president of the United States had been murdered, a president who in just 1,000 days in office had become beloved by the nation and the world.

"Charm the Birds Right Out of the Trees"

John F. Kennedy, born on May 29, 1917, was the second of nine children in an Irish-Catholic family from Brookline, Massachusetts. John had a happy childhood, but he was thin and often sick. He seemed to live in the shadow of his older brother, Joe.

Jack's mother, Rose Kennedy, was the daughter of a mayor of Boston. His father, Joe senior, was a wealthy businessman who would serve as ambassador to Great Britain. He was tough and taught his children to be competitive in school and in sports. Joe senior never let them forget that winning was enormously important.

Jack went to a private school where he was well-liked. He had a smile that people said could "charm the birds right out of the trees." He was not a particularly good student. He loved to play pranks and goof off. But after entering Harvard, Jack became serious about his studies and graduated with honors. He even wrote a book that became a best-seller, *Why England Slept*, which explained why that nation was so ill-prepared for World War II.

Jack enlisted in the navy in World War II. He became an officer and commanded a powerful little torpedo boat, *PT 109*. In 1943, it was rammed by a Japanese destroyer and cut in half. Jack was flung across the deck on his back, but he picked himself up and rallied his men. After jumping from the sinking ship, Kennedy swam for hours and rescued at least one crewman. For this act of heroism, Jack was awarded a medal for bravery, but his back injury plagued him for the rest of his life.

Jack's brother Joe, a navy pilot whom his father hoped would one day be president, was killed on a dangerous flying mission. The Kennedy family was devastated. From that time on Joe senior pinned all his hopes for the presidency on Jack and pressured him to go into politics.

The White House Rang with Children's Laughter

After the war, Jack was elected to the House of Representatives and served three terms. Then, in 1952, he won a seat in the Senate. Soon the Senate gallery was full of young women who came to watch the rich and handsome young congressman.

At a party, he met Jacqueline Bouvier, a stunning young woman who was working as a photographer. When she went to England to work, Jack waged an intense long-distance courtship and they were married in 1953 in Newport, Rhode Island, in one of the most glamorous weddings ever held. The bride was exquisite in a taffeta wedding dress and the groom looked handsome except for the red scratches on his face. (The day before, during a touch football game, he had fallen into a briar patch!) The Kennedys later had two children, Caroline and John junior, but lost a baby, Patrick, in infancy.

JFK won a close race for the presidency against Richard Nixon. He was inaugurated on January 20, 1961, at the age of forty-three, the youngest president ever to be elected. He was also the first chief executive to be born in the twentieth century, and the first Roman Catholic ever elected to the presidency.

During Kennedy's time in office, the White House rang with children's laughter. Caroline rode her pony, Macaroni, on the White House grounds and went to nursery school with friends in the family quarters. The family had several dogs. One of Caroline's favorites was Pushinka, a puppy given to her by the Soviet Union. The little dog's mother had been the first dog in space. Caroline's younger brother, John, played under his father's desk in the Oval Office and toddled from room to room clinging to his father's hand. Jackie, who was very interested in history, busied herself restoring the White House to its earlier grandeur, placing American period pieces, French antiques, and valuable art objects in the historic rooms.

As president, Kennedy faced down the Russians, forcing them to remove their missiles from Cuba, a country just off Florida's coast. He signed a treaty with England and Russia that banned nuclear testing in Earth's atmosphere. He also created the Peace Corps; pushed for a strong space program; and supported the arts, inviting writers, singers, actors, architects, and painters to the White House.

Doing Nothing

Caroline and John junior were the joy of Kennedy's life, and he loved having them nearby when he was working. Several times a day, he would come out of the Oval Office and clap his hands, and the children and their friends would come running. Kennedy loved to show his kids off to visitors and would let people photograph them when Jackie was not around.

One day when she was about three years old, Caroline was wandering around the White House when someone asked her, "Where's your daddy?"

"Oh, he's upstairs with his shoes and socks off, doing nothing," Caroline replied.

Then the chief executive and his wife went to Dallas on what was supposed to be an uneventful trip.

After John Fitzgerald Kennedy was assassinated by Lee Harvey Oswald, a pall fell over the world. People on the street huddled in small groups; others stayed by their televisions and radios for more news of the tragedy that seemed impossible to believe. Even today, anyone who lived through that horrifying time can tell you exactly where they were and what they were doing when they heard that John F. Kennedy had been shot.

Jackie's courage during the tragedy of her husband's murder won her the admiration of the world. But she felt that the American public would not give her and the children the privacy she needed. She moved to New York City and later married Aristotle Onassis, a wealthy Greek businessman. Following his death, and after Caroline and John had become adults, she worked as a book editor in New York. She died on May 19, 1994, and, along with President John F. Kennedy, is buried at Arlington Cemetery overlooking the Potomac River.

☆ Visit the ☆ JOHN F. KENNEDY Library and Museum

Soon after JFK's death, Jackie began planning the John Fitzgerald Kennedy Library and Museum. She chose the award-winning architect I. M. Pei as its designer. Dedicated in 1979, the building is situated on Columbia Point on Dorchester Bay, overlooking Boston's harbor and skyline. JFK's 26-foot sloop, *Victura*, is cradled on the lawn facing the water.

Twenty-five dramatic museum exhibits trace JFK's presidency, from his nomination to the White House years. Rare film and television footage, historic presidential documents, personal family keepsakes, and priceless gifts from world leaders give you a firsthand experience of President John F. Kennedy's life, leadership, and legacy.

You'll also enjoy seeing the famous televised White House tour Jackie gave the nation after its restoration. The president's birthplace is only a half hour's drive from the Kennedy Library.

The John F. Kennedy Library and Museum is in Boston, Massachusetts. Open daily, except New Year's Day, Thanksgiving, and Christmas, 9 A.M. to 5 P.M. Adults $5. Student discounts. For more information: Kennedy Library and Museum, Columbia Point, Boston, MA 92125. Telephone: 617-929-4523. Web site: http://www.cs.umb.edu/jfklibrary/museum.htm

Lyndon Baines Johnson

Lyndon Baines Johnson was sworn into office as president of the United States aboard *Air Force One* as it sat on the tarmac in Dallas, Texas. Earlier that day, a sniper's bullets had killed President John F. Kennedy. Vice President Johnson took the oath flanked by two women: the president's young widow, who stood frozen with grief, and Johnson's wife, Lady Bird, whose sad face echoed the feelings of the entire nation. In a matter of minutes the United States had a new president, one whose overwhelming concern for the poor led to his Great Society programs.

He Was Always Talking

Lyndon Baines Johnson was born in a farmhouse near Stonewall, Texas, on August 27, 1908. His family didn't have much money, but compared to their neighbors, the Johnsons were considered well-off even though they did not have electricity or running water.

Early every morning his father awakened the little boy with this summons, "Get up, Lyndon, every boy in town has already gotten an hour's start on you and you will never catch up." Lyndon did well in school except for deportment (conduct). He was always talking, a habit he never stopped! And he liked to be in charge. Although he often played with older children, he was usually the leader.

Sam Johnson, his father, served in the Texas legislature for ten years, so Lyndon learned about politics early. When he was ten, he got a job shining shoes at the Cecil Maddox Barbershop, where the local men gathered to get their hair cut and talk politics. Since the shop was the only place in Johnson City (the nearest large town) that received a newspaper, Lyndon usually hurried to his job early so he could sit in one of the tall barber chairs and read the news to the assembled crowd.

About this time, his grandfather wrote a letter to a friend saying, "I have a very fine grandson, smart as you can get them. I expect him to be a United States senator before he is forty." (Lyndon almost made it. In 1948, he became a U.S. senator at the age of forty.)

During Lyndon's childhood, Sam often took Lyndon to the capital with him. There the little boy learned to imitate his father, wearing a big Stetson and walking with long proud strides. He also started imitating his father's way of talking. Sam Johnson would put his arm around a man's shoulder, then look intently into his eyes. Soon Lyndon, too, was nailing people with his gaze and standing on tiptoe to put his arm around their shoulders!

Lyndon graduated from high school when he was fifteen years old. He went to California, where he picked oranges, washed cars and dishes, and did other odd jobs until he grew homesick. He returned to Texas and took a job on a road-building gang. He soon decided that he didn't want to do manual labor for the rest of his life. So at eighteen, he enrolled in Southwest Texas State Teachers College. He was an outstanding student and a member of the debate team, while also working to support himself.

After finishing school, he taught poor Mexican American students in the south Texas town of Cotulla. Lyndon did everything he could to help them. He often bought them food and athletic supplies out of his meager salary, but most of all he tried to give them a good education, so they could better themselves.

An Immediate Success

Lyndon left teaching to go to Washington, D.C., as Congressman Richard Kleberg's assistant. The young man was an immediate success, showing initiative, energy, and intelligence in his job.

On a trip home to Texas in 1934, he met Claudia Alta Taylor, the daughter of a wealthy landowner and businessman. He decided that he wanted to marry the soft-spoken Texas girl, who went by the nickname of "Lady Bird." Never one to hesitate, Lyndon took her for a car ride the first day they met and proposed marriage the next day.

Lady Bird refused then, but she accepted two months later and they were married the same year. They would eventually have two daughters, Lynda Bird and Luci Baines. (Father, mother, and daughters all had the initials LBJ.)

These were the years of the Great Depression, and President Roosevelt appointed Johnson as the director of the Texas National Youth Administration, a program designed to put unemployed young people to work. In 1937, he was elected to the House of Representatives. In 1941, Congressman Johnson served in World War II. Following the war, he won a Senate seat.

Great Society Program

Lyndon served three terms as one of the Democratic party's most influential leaders. In 1960, he became vice president under John Kennedy, then suddenly became president following JFK's assassination. LBJ was elected by a large majority in 1964 and launched his Great Society program, a program designed to help Americans who could not help themselves.

During Johnson's presidency, more civil rights laws were passed than at any other time since Abraham Lincoln. Segregation in all public

First Dogs

When the Johnsons moved into the White House, they had a pair of beagles named Him and Her. The two dogs were photographed almost as often as the president himself. Johnson caused an uproar when he was pictured picking up the dogs by their ears. Dog lovers all over the nation protested, saying the president was being cruel to the animals. Johnson replied that they liked it and people who worked at the White House said that the beagles did not seem to mind!

facilities was eliminated. He established Head Start and the Job Corps to help young people, extended Medicare for the elderly, and set up the Community Action program to aid the poor.

Although Lady Bird was shy, she was the most active First Lady since Eleanor Roosevelt. She made speeches all over the United States to push LBJ's antipoverty programs, but she also had her own agenda. She worked hard on passage of the Highway Beautification Act, which restricted billboards along highways. She was also successful in establishing gardens and parks in Washington, D.C. She worked tirelessly to preserve and reseed native wildflowers, grasses, shrubs, and trees. Her Secret Service agents muttered good-naturedly about Lady Bird's "walks in weeds," as they wiped the dirt and grass from their well-polished shoes after following her across the countryside.

LBJ inherited the Vietnam War, and although he personally disapproved of it, he could find no way out of the mess. Regardless of his personal views, he became so unpopular with many Americans over the issue that he chose not to run for a second elected term.

He returned to his Texas ranch, began his memoirs, and plunged into plans for the Lyndon Baines Johnson Library. After suffering from a heart ailment for several years, LBJ died on January 22, 1973. He is buried in the family plot at the LBJ ranch not far from Austin. He is survived by Lady Bird and their two daughters and grandchildren. Lady Bird is still active in her volunteer activities, LBJ's library, and her business interests.

"Watusi Luci"

When the Johnsons moved to the White House, their older daughter, Lynda Bird, was a student at the University of Texas in Austin. Luci Baines, their younger daughter, was sixteen years old. Like most teenagers, she wanted to be independent and often tried unsuccessfully to lose her Secret Service agents and get out on her own. The people who worked at the White House called her "Watusi Luci," after a popular dance she loved to do.

☆ Visit the ☆ LYNDON BAINES JOHNSON Library

The Lyndon Baines Johnson Library sits on the grounds of the University of Texas. The impressive eight-story marble building stands on a knoll overlooking the rest of the campus. It is the most visited of all the presidential libraries.

The library houses the papers and memorabilia of four decades of LBJ's public service. In the Great Hall, with its marble staircase, four stories of glass wall hold row upon row of red manuscript boxes stamped with the gold presidential seal. Other items of special interest include: a sword encrusted with diamonds; a rock from the moon; a fading letter from Franklin Roosevelt; a small slip of paper dated April 13, 1865, and signed "A. Lincoln"; and a ship's passport signed by President Thomas Jefferson. There's also a gift from Henry Ford II: a spunky little 1910 Model T Ford like the one that had belonged to the Sam Johnson family.

The Lyndon B. Johnson Library is in Austin, Texas. Open daily, except New Year's Day, Thanksgiving, and Christmas, 9 A.M. to 5 P.M. Admission is free. For more information: Lyndon B. Johnson Library, 2313 Red River, Austin, TX 78705. Telephone: 512-916-5137. Web site: http://www.lbjlib.utexas.edu

Richard Milhous Nixon

Richard M. Nixon was the most controversial political leader in U.S. history. He was a poor boy who rose steadily through the ranks of the Republican party, but his accomplishments in domestic and foreign affairs were overshadowed by the scandal of Watergate. Richard Nixon's many positive characteristics were often hard to see because of his stubborn and unforgiving nature. After leaving the presidency in disgrace, he worked hard to restore his reputation and became known for his books on foreign policy.

Winning Was Everything

Our thirty-seventh president was born in Yorba Linda, California, on January 9, 1913, the second of five boys. His mother was a former schoolteacher and his father owned a citrus grove that never seemed to make any money. People who knew the family said that Mr. Nixon was a hot-tempered man who was rough on his children.

When Richard was nine years old, his father sold the orange grove and opened a neighborhood market, where the whole family worked. Richard and his brothers swept the floors, boxed groceries, stocked the shelves, and, when they were older, got up at 4:00 A.M. every day to drive into Los Angeles to buy fresh produce.

To young Richard, winning was everything. He had relentless energy and was an excellent student. He made As in every subject and was especially good at memorizing and reciting poetry. Even as a child he was interested in politics, read newspapers, and loved to discuss current events. By the time he reached high school, he was a skilled debater and was active in hordes of school activities.

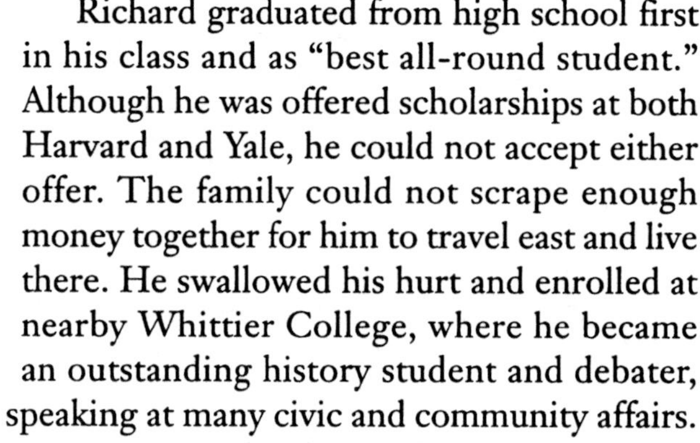

Richard graduated from high school first in his class and as "best all-round student." Although he was offered scholarships at both Harvard and Yale, he could not accept either offer. The family could not scrape enough money together for him to travel east and live there. He swallowed his hurt and enrolled at nearby Whittier College, where he became an outstanding history student and debater, speaking at many civic and community affairs.

He went to Duke University Law School and when he graduated, he joined a law firm in California. He met his future wife, Pat, when she was cast opposite him in a little theater group production of a play called *The Dark Tower.*

Pat (Thelma Catherine Ryan) was a pretty young schoolteacher who had worked her way through the University of Southern California and graduated with honors. The third time Nixon saw her, he told the surprised Pat that he wanted to marry her. She just laughed, but they began dating. After two years she gave in and became his wife.

By this time, World War II had started, and Nixon joined the navy. He served as an officer in the South Pacific, although he never saw combat. He later jokingly said that the most dangerous things he faced during that time were "giant, stinging centipedes."

The "Checkers" Speech

After the war, a group of Republican businessmen persuaded the young lawyer to run for Congress. Nixon won the election after running a race that his supporters called aggressive, but many others said it was dishonest and underhanded.

Nixon ran for the Senate against Democrat Helen Gahagan Douglas, who was also a member of the House. He called Representative Douglas a Communist sympathizer without ever offering proof. He also told voters that women should be at home, not in the Senate.

Nixon won the campaign, one of the dirtiest and most dishonest in history, for which he was nicknamed "Tricky Dick."

In 1952, Dwight Eisenhower ran for the presidency with Nixon as his running mate, but Nixon was almost taken off the ticket when he was accused of having a secret "slush fund" of $18,000. Immediately, Nixon appeared on television to explain that the fund was not secret; he had simply not mentioned it since he figured nobody was interested. He told the nation that he had accepted only one gift, a black-and-white cocker spaniel that his daughters named "Checkers," and he warned the nation that the girls weren't about to give the dog back! The next day, dog lovers from around the nation sent Nixon 300,000 favorable letters and phone calls. This television address became known as the "Checkers" speech.

At the end of Eisenhower's terms of office, Nixon ran for president but lost to John F. Kennedy. Nixon moved back to California and ran for governor, but he lost that race, too. Bitter over the losses, he moved to New York City to lick his wounds and regroup. In 1967, however, he won the presidential race, but his vice president, Spiro Agnew, would resign while in office for accepting bribes. Nixon's first term was also plagued by economic problems and unrest about the Vietnam War. On the plus side, his first term was marked by successes in foreign affairs when he went to the Republic of China and to the Soviet Union. The Vietnam War was also finally grinding to a halt.

Pat Nixon often said that "the role of a politician's wife was not one I would have chosen." When Nixon decided to go into politics, she asked for two promises from him: that she would never be asked to make a political speech, and that their home would remain a quiet place for the

Julie's Wedding

When Julie Nixon married David Eisenhower (Ike's grandson), she was the eighth woman to be married at the White House. She wanted the guest list to remain short, but more and more people were invited. Finally, her mother half-seriously suggested that they toss all the names in the air and invite only those who landed faceup! The wedding, held in the Rose Garden, turned out to be simple but spectacular. Although Julie marked some names off the list, she did invite the three living White House brides, Luci Baines Johnson, Lynda Bird Johnson, and Alice Longworth Roosevelt. (The other brides were Elizabeth Tyler, Frances Folsom, Nellie Wrenshall Grant, and Jessie Woodrow Wilson.)

family, not a place for "political stunts" or political meetings. Nixon agreed to both promises. As a result, their two daughters, Patricia ("Tricia") and Julie, led as private a life as their devoted parents could make it while Nixon was president.

The Watergate Scandal

Nixon was reelected in 1972. During the campaign, a group of Nixon supporters had burglarized Democratic party headquarters at the Watergate building in Washington, D.C., and planted an illegal listening device to get campaign information. It later came out that the president had authorized the payment of $40,000 to the burglars. The Watergate scandal brought to light a long list of political misdoings of the Nixon administration.

For two years Nixon frantically tried to cover up what he'd done, but it was impossible. The details of his involvement in the scandal surfaced and he faced impeachment. He resigned, a man who had betrayed the trust of the American people and disgraced the presidency. He later said, "I let the American people down. And I have to carry that burden with me the rest of my life."

After his resignation in 1974, he and Pat returned to their seaside home in San Clemente, California, where he began his autobiography. During this time he confided to friends, "I don't intend to fade away." He and Pat moved to New Jersey to be closer to their daughters and grandchildren, but also to be closer to the seat of government. Over the next decade Nixon gradually became a spokesman on international affairs until his death in 1994.

The "Enemies" List

Nixon seemed to think that everyone was out to get him. He had his staff keep a list of "enemies," which included not only political figures but entertainers, such as Bill Cosby and Jane Fonda, and athletes, such as quarterback Joe Namath. Nixon had FBI Director J. Edgar Hoover try to collect damaging information about these and other people by using illegal wiretaps.

☆ Visit the ☆ RICHARD M. NIXON Library and Birthplace

The Richard M. Nixon Library and Birthplace occupies 9 acres in Yorba Linda, California. It encompasses twenty-two presidential museum galleries, movie and interactive video theaters, the First Lady's flower garden, the modest frame house where Nixon was born, and the burial place of the former president and his wife.

One of the most fascinating exhibits is the limousine that transported Presidents Johnson, Nixon, Ford, and Carter throughout the world. A gift from the Ford Motor Company, the sleek bullet-proof automobile is a luxurious "rolling fortress." The *Guinness Book of World Records* calls the special Lincoln Continental "the most expensive car ever built."

The Richard M. Nixon Library and Birthplace is in Yorba Linda, California. Open daily, except New Year's Day, Thanksgiving, and Christmas, Monday through Saturday, 10 A.M. to 5 P.M., Sunday 11 A.M. to 5 P.M. Adults $4.50, children 7 and under free. For more information: Nixon Library, 1800 Yorba Linda Boulevard, Yorba Linda, CA 92686. Telephone: 714-993-3393. Web site: http://www.nixonfoundation.org/

Gerald Rudolph Ford

Gerald R. Ford was the first American to replace both a resigned vice president and a resigned president, following two of the worst scandals in this nation's history. He replaced Spiro Agnew as vice president to Richard Nixon when Agnew was accused of accepting bribes. Then during one of this country's darkest periods, he replaced the disgraced Richard Nixon as president after the crimes of Watergate. Ford's decency and moral character helped heal the nation after these two crippling blows.

He Would Look for the Best in Everybody

He was born Leslie Lynch King, Jr., in Omaha, Nebraska, on July 14, 1913. A year after his birth, his parents were divorced and his mother and Leslie returned to Grand Rapids, Michigan, to live with her parents. Four years later, the young woman remarried, and her new husband adopted Leslie. They changed the little boy's name to Gerald Rudolph Ford after his stepfather.

Three more children were born and Jerry took a great deal of responsibility for the household. Rising at 6:00 A.M., he took care of the furnace, helped with the cooking, and washed dishes before going to school each morning.

Jerry was a good student in grade school, but he had a hot temper and got into lots of fights. After he started high school, Jerry's philosophy of life began to develop. He decided that most people had more good qualities than bad and that he would look for the best in everybody. As a result of this attitude, Jerry made and kept many friends.

He grew into a big kid who loved to play sports. When he was a sophomore, he went out for football and became a star, winning a place on the all-city squad. His team captured the state championship.

During his last year of high school, he won a contest as the most popular senior in all the high schools of Grand Rapids. The prize was a five-day trip to Washington, D.C. Jerry had a great time and enjoyed visiting Congress and the White House, but he never dreamed he would be president of the United States one day.

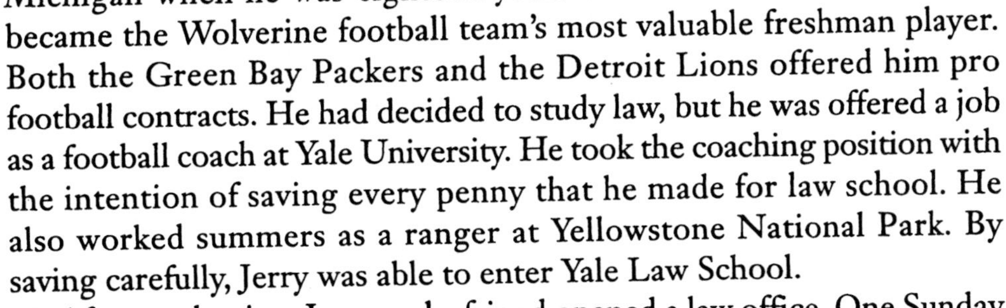

He won a scholarship to the University of Michigan when he was eighteen years old and became the Wolverine football team's most valuable freshman player. Both the Green Bay Packers and the Detroit Lions offered him pro football contracts. He had decided to study law, but he was offered a job as a football coach at Yale University. He took the coaching position with the intention of saving every penny that he made for law school. He also worked summers as a ranger at Yellowstone National Park. By saving carefully, Jerry was able to enter Yale Law School.

After graduating, Jerry and a friend opened a law office. One Sunday evening, listening to the car radio on the way home, Jerry heard an excited voice announce that the Japanese had bombed Pearl Harbor. Jerry joined the navy and by November 1943 was in heavy combat in the Pacific. After forty-seven months, he was mustered out of the service as a lieutenant commander who had won many medals.

A "Team Player"

Back in civilian life, Jerry joined a law firm in Grand Rapids, Michigan. He also volunteered his services to many worthy causes and wanted to become involved in government. He ran for Congress in 1948 and won the election.

Jerry had been engaged to be married when he was in college, but his fiancée had broken it off. Since then he hadn't wanted to get serious about any woman. Then he met Betty Warren, a fashion coordinator at a local store. She was recently divorced and also didn't want to become seriously involved with anyone.

As a teenager, Betty Ford had been a model. She later studied under the great dancer and choreographer Martha Graham, and she became a member of Ms. Graham's dance troupe. Betty and Jerry started dating and were married in 1948. They would have four children: a daughter, Susan, and three sons, Michael, John, and Steven.

The Fords moved to Washington, D.C., when Jerry became a congressman. A moderate Republican, the tall, handsome Jerry was quickly seen to be a "team player." He became close friends with Richard Nixon, then a congressman from California, when they sat on an important committee together.

In 1973, when Vice President Spiro Agnew resigned in a storm of scandal, Ford was chosen to be the new vice president. Every day brought more damaging revelations about White House and presidential involvement in the Watergate scandal. Then in 1974, rather than accepting impeachment, Richard Nixon resigned and Jerry Ford became president.

A "Challenge"

Few presidents have faced such a mess, or as Ford chose to call it, a "challenge." The country's economy was crippled and unemployment was high. Perhaps Ford's greatest accomplishment was establishing trust in the office of the presidency. Historians say his greatest political mistake was to pardon Richard Nixon, since the majority of Americans felt the former president should be punished.

As First Lady, Betty Ford expressed herself with humor and honesty, which endeared her to people. She sometimes admitted to "putting her foot in her mouth," but Americans loved her for it. When she was diagnosed with breast cancer, she chose to make it public. Her honesty about her illness and the resulting surgery is credited with saving many women's lives. Later, she admitted her alcohol and drug abuse, making public her struggle to control it. After spending time in hospital rehabilitation, she

Our Most Athletic President

At sixty-two, Gerald Ford was our most athletic president. He was in splendid physical shape and swam, skied, and played golf and tennis. But on a trip to Austria, he got his shoe caught on the ramp of *Air Force One* and fell to the tarmac. He jumped up unhurt, but to his surprise, newspaper reporters made a big deal of it. Later that day his foot slipped twice on a rain-slick staircase and a legend was born: President Ford was clumsy. After that, every time Ford bumped his head, fell on a ski slope, or stumbled, reporters told the world. Comedians poked fun at the president, but he was usually a good sport, grinning and taking the jokes with good humor.

established the Betty Ford Center in Palm Springs, where she is still active.

When Ford took office, his youngest child, Susan, was a teenager. Susan remembers that it was like living in a fairy tale, but that sometimes the White House was a cross between a convent and a prison. The members of the press corps did not approve of her wearing jeans. The sixteen-year-old also did not like having her Secret Service bodyguard going along on her dates. But she had her senior prom at the White House. She also had opportunities to meet movie stars and celebrities and lots of "just plain people that I never would have met if my father had not been president."

☆ Visit the ☆ GERALD R. FORD Museum and Library

The Gerald R. Ford Museum and Library are separated by 130 miles.

The museum, a triangular granite and glass structure, overlooks a city park and river in Grand Rapids. One of the most interesting exhibits is the little surplus World War II building, called a Quonset hut, which housed Ford's campaign headquarters when he first ran for Congress. Other fascinating displays include a replica of the Oval Office as it was in Ford's administration. An electronic device allows you to activate and "enter" different White House rooms. One interesting exhibit lets you join the president of France, Clint Eastwood, Martha Graham, and Mrs. Ford at their table during a state dinner.

The library and archives are on the campus of the University of Michigan at Ann Arbor, Ford's alma mater. Here scholars can work with nearly 20 million historical papers and audiovisual materials.

The Gerald R. Ford Museum is in Grand Rapids, Michigan. Open daily, except New Year's Day, Thanksgiving, and Christmas, 9 A.M. to 5 P.M. Adults $4, children under 16 free. For more information: The Gerald R. Ford Museum, 303 Pearl Street NW, Grand Rapids, MI 49504-5353. Telephone: 616-451-9263. The Gerald R. Ford Library is in Ann Arbor, MI. Open for research Monday through Friday, except federal holidays, 8:45 A.M. to 4:45 P.M. For more information: The Gerald R. Ford Library, 1000 Beal Avenue, Ann Arbor, MI 48109. Telephone: 734-741-2218. Web site for both institutions: http://www.lbjlib.utexas.edu/ford/

James Earl Carter, Jr.

Jimmy Carter, our thirty-ninth president, was a political outsider from Georgia with little government experience. What he did have was a focused energy and absolute honesty and integrity, which appealed to a nation still recovering from Watergate. Unfortunately, these wonderful qualities may have worked against him during his term of office, but they've made him one of our finest statesmen as an ex-president.

He Liked to Fish

James Earl Carter, Jr., was born in Plains, Georgia, on October 1, 1924. The first U.S. president born in a hospital, Jimmy was the eldest of four children. His father was a prosperous peanut farmer and his mother, "Miss Lillian," was a registered nurse.

Jimmy was a good boy, but he was far from perfect. One time Jimmy shot his sister Gloria with a BB gun after she threw a wrench at him. Another time, after Jimmy was selected as valedictorian of his high school graduating class, he played hooky, got caught, and was denied the honor.

Jimmy studied hard and was an avid reader. He also played tennis, ran track, and played baseball and basketball, but most of all he liked to fish. His best fishing pal was Rachel Clark, an African American girl who could outfish almost anyone! She would go fishing with Jimmy only if he dug up the earthworms for bait. After he had filled a can with worms, they would walk 5 miles to the Choctawhatchee or Kinchafoonee Creek and catch their limits of perch or bass. Later, Jimmy Carter would remember these as some of the happiest times of his life.

From the time he was six years old, Jimmy wanted to go to the U.S. Naval Academy. His uncle was in the navy and sent him postcards and gifts from all over the world. Jimmy's worst fear was that he wouldn't be accepted at the Naval Academy. He worried that he might not be able to pass the physical examination because he had flat feet. While he was in high school, Jimmy spent hours rolling his feet over Coke bottles, hoping to correct the defect.

After a year in college, he was awarded an appointment to the U.S. Naval Academy. He loved the school, but it was tough. One night when Jimmy was a senior at Annapolis and at home on leave, he asked Rosalynn Smith, a pretty seventeen-year-old friend of his sister's, for a date. When he got home that night, he told his mother, "Rosalynn is the girl I want to marry" and he did, as soon as he graduated.

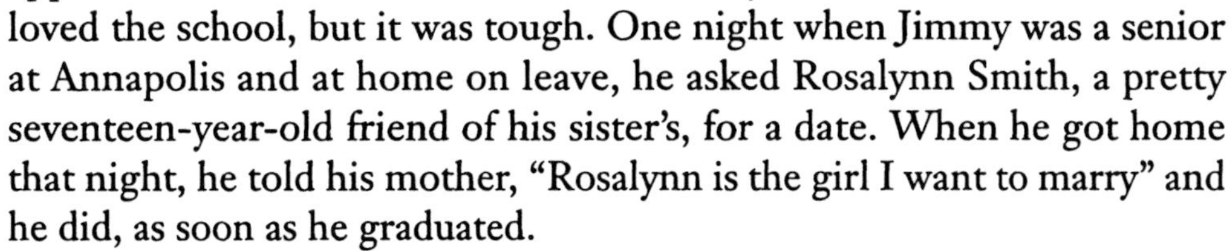

Jimmy served on many battleships, but in time he wanted a change and transferred to the submarine fleet. The young officer won admission to the navy's new nuclear submarine program and served under Admiral Hyman Rickover, one of the toughest but most admired men in the fleet. Carter soon became senior officer of the *Sea Wolf*, the second U.S. nuclear sub.

When his father died, Jimmy left the navy to run the family peanut business back in Plains, Georgia. With Rosalynn's help managing business accounts and by introducing modern methods, the young couple saved the ailing business, although their first year's profit was

President of What?

Most people, including his mother, were surprised when Jimmy Carter ran for president. When he told Miss Lillian in the summer of 1974 that he was planning to run for president, she asked, "President of what, Jimmy?"

only $184! Rosalynn and Jimmy had four children: John William, James Earl III (Chip), Donnel Jeffery, and Amy Lynn.

During this time, Miss Lillian, in her sixties and no bored grandma, surprised the family by joining the Peace Corps. The Carters worried about her, but trying to stop Miss Lillian once she'd made up her mind was utterly useless. She put on her nurse's oxfords once more and went to India, where she worked in a family-planning clinic.

Camp David Peace Accords

Egypt and Israel had been at war since 1948 when Jimmy Carter invited Anwar Sadat and Menachem Begin to Camp David to negotiate peace talks. At the isolated presidential retreat in Maryland, with Carter acting as negotiator, Egypt's Sadat and Israel's Begin came to an historic agreement and signed a peace treaty in March 1979.

He Championed Human Rights

Jimmy won a seat in the Georgia state senate in 1962 and became governor of Georgia in 1970. By 1974, he was becoming better known in national Democratic circles, but when he decided to run for the presidency, many considered it a joke or a way of holding the spot for a more successful party candidate. But soon people who had asked "Jimmy who?" when Carter's name was mentioned began to take him seriously. At the Democratic convention Carter impressed the delegates with his knowledge of issues and outperformed better-known Washington leaders. The presidential race against incumbent Gerald R. Ford was one of the closest in U.S. history, but Carter won.

Jimmy Carter served one term as president from 1977 to 1981. In office, he championed human rights around the world. Rosalynn was her husband's closest adviser and even attended cabinet meetings. She was a skilled speaker and a hardworking First Lady.

Amy was nine years old when the Carters moved to the White House. Unlike many presidential children, Amy attended public school. She often brought friends home to play in her tree house. She had a dog named Grits and a cat called Misty Malarky Ying Yang.

Once when her father was taking her to the zoo, she ran up to her mother's room to ask for a pencil to take along. When Rosalynn asked why she needed a pencil at the zoo, Amy replied, "To sign autographs."

The most difficult problem Carter faced as president was the kidnapping of U.S. embassy employees in Iran. Carter would not give in to the terrorists' demands. Negotiations continued and an airborne rescue attempt failed. Many people felt that Carter was not tough enough to handle the situation, but he did not want to endanger the lives of the hostages. Carter's campaign for reelection was conducted under the continued shadow of threats to kill the hostages.

Ronald Reagan won the election and the hostages were released on the day he was inaugurated. Carter spent the first day of his retirement greeting the hostages in a hospital in West Germany.

The Carters returned to Georgia to find that their business had gone downhill during their absence. Once more, Jimmy and Rosalynn started building the business back up again, but they also worked hard for many humanitarian causes. The couple established the Carter Center in Atlanta, a nonprofit, nonpartisan institution dedicated to fighting hunger, poverty, disease, conflict, and oppression around the world. The Carters are also volunteers for Habitat for Humanity, an organization that helps the needy in the United States and other countries renovate or build homes for themselves.

☆ Visit the ☆ CARTER CENTER

The Carter Center, including a library and museum, is located in a wooded park of 35 acres, just five minutes from downtown Atlanta. The grounds are spectacular, with a rose garden, a wildflower meadow, a Japanese garden, waterfalls, a cherry orchard, and two small lakes.

The museum houses many exhibits that offer an overview of the presidency, including a replica of the Oval Office. Through a video display called "Town Meeting," the visitor can enter a dialogue with the former president. Many state gifts that were presented to the Carters are on display, including a stunning silver falcon from the Kingdom of Saudi Arabia, and a gold evening purse studded with diamonds, rubies, and onyx. The inaugural gowns worn by Rosalynn Carter and other First Ladies, and a formal dinner setting from the White House, are also displayed.

The Carter Center is in Atlanta, Georgia. Open Monday through Friday, except New Year's Day, Thanksgiving, and Christmas, 9 A.M. to 4:45 P.M. Adults $4, children under 16 free. For more information: Carter Presidential Center, One Copenhill Avenue, Atlanta, GA 30307. Telephone: 404-331-3900. Web site: http://www.CarterCenter.org/

Ronald Wilson Reagan

Ronald Reagan, a former movie star, was one of the most popular U.S. presidents. Although the oldest ever elected at sixty-nine, he sometimes seemed much younger. Like Theodore Roosevelt, Reagan really appeared to enjoy his time in office. He has been called the "Great Communicator" because he was a good speaker with a gift for inspiring trust.

The Start of His Successful Acting Career

Ronald was born in Tampico, Illinois, on February 6, 1911, in a cramped apartment above the general store on Main Street. His mother was a strong woman with midwestern values that she instilled in "Dutch" (Ronald's nickname) and his younger brother, whose nickname was "Moon." The boys' father was a charming man but an alcoholic. The family moved from place to place but finally settled in Dixon, Illinois, when Dutch was nine years old.

Since the family was poor, it was necessary for each member to work. Mrs. Reagan took in sewing and sometimes clerked at a store. As a teenager, Dutch worked as a lifeguard. Although he was athletic, he was often dreamy and quiet. He loved to read and spent many hours in the public library. In school, he was elected class president.

He also acted in school plays, ran track, and played football and basketball.

Reagan attended Eureka College in Illinois, where he studied economics and sociology. He also played on the football team and became interested in campus politics and drama.

After graduation, Reagan went to work as a radio sports announcer. While Reagan was in California covering the Chicago Cubs' spring training in 1937, a Warner Brothers studio agent signed him for the part of a radio broadcaster in a movie. That role was the start of his successful acting career, which spanned over thirty years, and in which he made more than fifty films.

Reagan married an actress, Jane Wyman, in 1940 and settled down in California. They had two children, Maureen and Michael. While the children were young, the Reagans saw a house in the movie *This Thing Called Love* that they liked so well, they built a house just like it. They also had a pair of Scottie dogs named Scotch and Soda.

Reagan joined the army in 1942, but because of his extreme nearsightedness he never saw combat duty. Instead he made training films. Personal differences and work pressures led Ronald and Jane to divorce in 1949.

That same year, Reagan met a young actress named Nancy Davis, who shared his political views. Nancy had once answered a questionnaire by saying that her greatest ambition in life was to have a happy marriage. They were married in 1952 and soon had two children, Patricia ("Patti") and Ronald.

Ronald continued as an actor and then became a spokesman for the General Electric Company. In 1964, he made a television speech supporting Barry Goldwater for president, a speech that was said to have raised more contributions than any other single speech prior to that time.

BEDTIME FOR BONZO

In one Ronald Reagan movie, *Bedtime for Bonzo*, the future president's co-star was a chimpanzee. Years later, when someone showed the president a picture of himself in bed with Bonzo, Reagan quipped, "I'm the one wearing the watch."

California Republican leaders decided that Reagan was "governor material."

He ran for governor in 1966 and won. During this time, Reagan called himself a nonpolitician, blaming California's many troubles on other state and national politicians. He spent two terms as governor and then started looking toward the presidency.

"I Forgot to Duck"

Reagan won the Republican party's nomination and easily defeated Jimmy Carter in 1980. Two months after he became president, Reagan was walking toward his limousine after speaking in the Washington, D.C., Hilton Hotel. Suddenly, a man who had been standing nearby crouched and opened fire on the president. John Hinckley fired two shots, then four more. At the sound of the first innocent-sounding pop from the handgun, a Secret Service agent shoved Reagan through the open door of the armored limousine and the car screeched away to a hospital.

The president had been hit. Three others were also wounded in the assassination attempt, including Reagan's press secretary, James Brady. At the hospital, the doctors found that the bullet had punctured a lung and had come to rest just an inch from the president's heart. As doctors prepared him for surgery, Reagan joked, "I forgot to duck."

He made a remarkable recovery, and his wit and grace during this difficult time caused his popularity to soar. His assailant, Hinckley, did not have a political motive. He said that his act was a love offering for the actress Jodie Foster, whom he had never met.

Reagan became the first president since Eisenhower to serve two full terms. During that time, he dealt with the Iran-Contra scandal, in which the United States sold arms to Iran and some of the money was used to fund rebels in Nicaragua, as well as increased terrorism against Americans abroad. Still, his life in the White House remained pretty predictable. Nancy, who had once said that her life began when she met her husband, made his health and comfort her first priority. Reagan required a regular and predictable schedule, rising at 7:30 A.M. and going to bed at 10:30 or 11:00 P.M., and she saw that he got it. By most White House standards this was a leisurely existence, with weekends spent at Camp David and lots of other vacations.

Jelly Beans

When Ronald Reagan stopped smoking, he found it helpful to pop jelly beans into his mouth when he craved a cigarette. Soon, they got to be a habit. While he was the governor of California, he started bringing jars of jelly beans to meetings. Soon, his staff developed the jelly bean habit, too. Reagan later said they "got so they could hardly make a decision without passing the jelly beans around."

After his retirement in 1989, the Reagans returned to California. The former president still enjoyed horseback riding and clearing brush on his ranch in the hills above Santa Barbara. He also took part in planning his presidential library and made appearances and speeches, until he was diagnosed as having Alzheimer's disease.

☆ Visit the RONALD REAGAN Presidential Library and Museum ☆

The Ronald Reagan Presidential Library and Museum occupies a 29-acre site on a hilltop in the rolling foothills of Simi Valley, California. The low, rambling California Mission-style building with a red tile roof is built in a U shape, with long shady corridors that are usually cooled by the ocean breezes that blow inland. The site commands a view of rugged mountain ranges stretching as far as the eye can see, a view that is especially admired by both Nancy and Ronald Reagan.

Inside the museum, the visitor moves through permanent exhibits that follow Reagan's early years, his acting career, his time as California governor, and his presidency. Of special interest is a portrait of Reagan done entirely in butterflies' wings by craftsmen of the Central African Republic. Other unusual portraits of the former president are done in precious stones, seed beads, and jelly beans!

The last gallery, called "Meet President Reagan," features an audiotape of the former president discussing his toughest decisions, his radio and Hollywood days, his first date with Nancy, his life on the ranch, his political views, and many other subjects.

The Ronald Reagan Presidential Library and Museum is in Simi Valley, California. Open daily, except New Year's Day, Thanksgiving, and Christmas, Monday through Saturday 9 A.M. to 5 P.M., Sunday noon to 5 P.M. Adults $2, children 15 and under free. For more information: Presidential Library, 40 Presidential Drive, Simi Valley, CA 93065. Telephone: 805-522-8444. Web site: http://www.reagan.utexas.edu

George Herbert Walker Bush

George Bush stepped into the spotlight of the presidency in 1988, after eight years as vice president under Ronald Reagan. Bush was faced with many challenges. He had to deal with serious economic conditions, the problems of homelessness, the drug crisis, and educational and environmental issues.

"Have Half"

Born on June 12, 1924, in Milton, Massachusetts, George Herbert Walker Bush was the second son of a wealthy family. The family soon moved to Greenwich, Connecticut, and in the 1950s George's father became a Republican senator from that state.

Although George had three younger siblings, he and his older brother, Prescott, were especially close. They shared a bedroom, but their mother thought they might like separate rooms, so she had a wall built down the middle of the room. To her surprise they didn't seem very excited. For months she did not understand why the boys weren't happier about having their own spaces. Then, near Christmastime, the boys asked her for a special present: They wanted the wall removed so they could be together again.

All the Bush children were brought up to be generous, but of the five, George was the most unselfish with his things. In fact, everybody called him "Have Half." This strange nickname was given because he so often offered half of whatever he had to his brothers and sisters or playmates.

George was polite and friendly to all. He did well in school and quickly became a leader in sports. The boy was well coordinated and a natural at most games. He was also never afraid to show the tender side of his nature. Once on visitors' day at his school, during an exhibition of games an overweight boy got stuck going through a barrel and everybody started to laugh. But George's mother noticed that George was crying. He ran onto the field and helped the boy struggle out and then ran by his side for the rest of the race.

After graduating from Phillips Academy in Andover, Massachusetts, George planned to enter college, but the bombing of Pearl Harbor by the Japanese changed that. He joined the navy on his eighteenth birthday and became a pilot. He had a notable war record, receiving the Distinguished Flying Cross and three other medals for combat duty.

George and Barbara Pierce were married on January 6, 1945. The pair had gone steady since both were teenagers, but they didn't marry until his combat duty was over. Following the war, the young couple moved to New Haven where George entered Yale, his father's alma mater. George became one of the university's top athletes and graduated with academic honors.

After living in Odessa, Texas, and briefly in California, George, Barbara, and their young children, George and Robin, settled in Midland, Texas, where George was in the oil business. They lived in a neighborhood in which all the houses were alike, but each was painted a different bright color. The area was known as "Easter Egg Row," and the Bushes' house was an electric blue. It was a happy life until the Bushes' daughter, three-year-old Robin, developed leukemia and died. Family friends have said that twenty-eight-year-old Barbara's brown hair turned white during that sorrowful time.

After a period of deep grief, the Bushes had happy news. Barbara was pregnant again. In the next six years, they had four more children: John Ellis ("Jeb"), Neil Mallon, Marvin Pierce, and Dorothy ("Doro").

Wild Swings of Success and Failure

Within a decade after leaving Yale, George owned a successful offshore oil drilling business, but he was ready to move in another direction. He decided to enter politics as his father had done.

George served two terms in the House of Representatives, where he sat on several important committees. President Nixon appointed him the U.S. representative to the United Nations, a post he held for two years. Following that, he served as chairman of the Republican National Committee. Then Gerald Ford appointed Bush as chief of the U.S. Liaison Office in newly opened China and two years later made him head of the CIA. From there he became vice president under Ronald Reagan.

Eight years later, in 1988, George Bush was elected president of the United States. His administration was marked by wild swings of success and failure. Early in his term, Communism fell in Eastern Europe and Russia, bringing the long Cold War to an end. He ordered the successful Operation Desert Storm against Iraq, but at home, the country fell into a deep economic decline.

Barbara Bush's down-to-earth manner, warmth, and wit made her a very popular First Lady. Thoroughly familiar with capital social life after eight years as the vice president's wife, she was very comfortable in her role at the White House. In discussing her job as First Lady, she said, "I don't fool around with his [George's] office and he doesn't fool around with my household." She decided that her cause would be promoting literacy around the country.

Although the Bush children were adults when their father was elected president, there was another member of the family, Millie, the Bushes' English springer spaniel, that got almost as much publicity as a "White House kid." The little dog was especially big news when she gave birth to a litter of puppies at the White House and when—with Barbara's help—she wrote *Millie's Book*, whose earnings went to the literacy fund.

After only one term, George and Barbara left Washington, D.C., and returned to private life, spending part of their time in Houston, Texas, and part at their summer home in Maine.

Broccoli

George Bush was the first president to state publicly that he did not like broccoli. Many vegetable haters agreed with him, but broccoli growers around the world were furious! They sent truckloads of broccoli to the White House. The president graciously accepted the green gifts, but he said, "I'm the President of the United States and I do not have to eat it."

☆ Visit the ☆ GEORGE BUSH Presidential Library and Museum

This latest presidential library was dedicated in November 1997, with four of the five living presidents and their wives present. (Ronald Reagan was unable to attend.) Located on 90 acres in College Station, Texas, the library is situated in a grove of large oak trees bordering a running creek. Visitors enter the building of Texas granite and limestone through a semicircular 50-foot glass rotunda. Two wings branch off this lobby, one for exhibitions and another for archives. Notable exhibits include a *TBM Avenger* aircraft like the one Bush flew during World War II and a Studebaker car like the one he drove to Texas when he entered the oil business.

The library buildings also house a collection of official records from the Bush administration and countless personal papers from his career at the UN in China, at the CIA, and as president. Since Bush wanted this to be a facility for learning about government, three study centers are an important part of the library: the George Bush School of Government and Public Service, the Center of Presidential Studies, and the Center for Public Leadership Studies.

The George Bush Presidential Library and Museum is open Monday through Friday, 9:30 A.M. to 5 P.M., Saturday noon to 5 P.M. Adults $3, children under 16 free. For more information: The George Bush Presidential Library Center, Texas A&M University, College Station, TX 77843-1145. Telephone: 409-260-9552. Web site: http://www.csdl.tamu.edu/bushlib/

William Jefferson Clinton

Bill Clinton, the forty-second president of the United States, was called a "wonder boy" when, at the age of twenty-seven, he ran against a Republican congressman considered unbeatable. He didn't exactly defeat him, but he came very close. By the time he was thirty-four, people thought Bill Clinton was washed up when he was defeated for a second term as governor of Arkansas, becoming the youngest ex-governor in history. "The people sent me a message," he later said, "and I learned my lesson." William Jefferson Clinton learned his lesson well, for he bounced back to become Arkansas's governor for five terms and president of the United States for two.

His First Love Was Politics

Bill was born in Hope, Arkansas, three months after his father, William Jefferson Blythe III, was killed in an automobile accident. Bill lived with his grandparents, who owned a small grocery store, while his mother, Virginia, attended school in New Orleans to become a nurse-anesthetist. The young woman was heartbroken to leave her child. She and the little boy were both crying when she left by train for school, but Bill's grandmother told him, "She's doing this for you."

By the time Bill was four years old, his mother had finished her nurse's training and married Roger Clinton, and they were a family again. Then when Bill was ten years old, his half brother, Roger, was born. Bill loved the baby and took good care of him. In fact, the older boy changed his name to Clinton so Roger would have the same last name as his big brother when he started school. The family moved to Hot Springs, where Bill excelled in school. He was so sharp and intelligent that he always led the class.

However, all was not well at home. Bill's stepfather had a drinking problem. When he was drunk, he became abusive to his wife and younger son. Once he even fired a gun in the house. The teenage Bill did everything he could to protect his mother and brother. Finally, Bill stepped in front of his raging stepfather and told him, "You will never hit either one of them again. If you want them, you'll have to go through me." This stopped the abuse, but not the drinking.

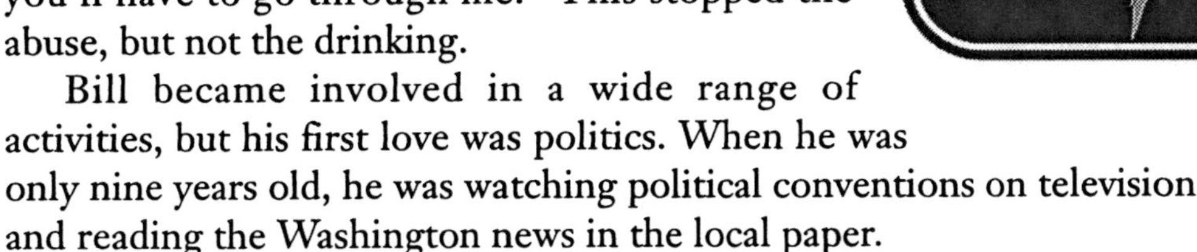

Bill became involved in a wide range of activities, but his first love was politics. When he was only nine years old, he was watching political conventions on television and reading the Washington news in the local paper.

The summer he was seventeen, he attended Boys' State, a program designed to teach students about politics and government. Following that, he was elected to Boys' Nation and traveled to Washington, D.C., to join other high school students in running a make-believe government. On this trip he met and shook hands with his idol, John F. Kennedy, an experience Clinton still treasures.

While attending Georgetown University, he worked part-time in the office of Senator William Fulbright of Arkansas to support himself. Following his graduation, Bill won a Rhodes scholarship that allowed him to study at Oxford University in England. After leaving Oxford, Bill won a scholarship to Yale Law School. Even with the scholarship, he still had to work three jobs to stay in school.

At Yale, he met Hillary Rodham, who was also a law student. The brilliant Hillary, who came from a prosperous Chicago family, was editor of the *Yale Law Review*. The two high-achieving law students dated steadily while in school but went to work in different parts of the country when they graduated: Bill to carve out a career in Arkansas politics and Hillary to Washington, D.C., to work in a government job.

Although the two were thousands of miles apart, they kept in touch. Then in 1974, Hillary began teaching at the University of Arkansas Law School to be near Bill. Their romance bloomed and Bill asked her to marry him. He told her, "I know this is really a hard choice for you since I'm committed to living in Arkansas." Although Hillary had plans for a law career that could have taken her all over the world, she decided to follow her heart. The pair were married in 1975 in a quiet ceremony.

BILL'S SAXOPHONE

Since grade school, Bill Clinton has loved to play the saxophone. His music teacher used to brag that the little boy "played the horn as tenderly as a violin." He occasionally still plays at public events, for example, at a recent birthday party for jazz great Lionel Hampton.

The Youngest Governor in the United States

Clinton's political career was well under way by the time he was twenty-seven. He enjoyed campaigning and people responded to his warmth. At thirty-two, he was the youngest governor in the United States.

Hillary was a member of a law firm in Little Rock and later became the first woman to make partner in that firm. On a visit to England Bill and Hillary enjoyed a beautiful morning in the Chelsea section of London. Flowers were blooming and the sun was shining as they walked hand in hand. The two were so happy at that time that when their daughter was born on February 27, 1980, they named her Chelsea Victoria.

Clinton entered the Arkansas governor's office eager to bring about reform, but many people in the state thought he was trying to move too fast. Some were even angry that the governor's wife had kept her maiden name. He became very unpopular and was not reelected.

But in 1982, a more mature Bill Clinton regained the governorship and served until 1992. By now he was also drawing national attention and won the presidential election in 1992.

The Challenges of the White House

After his election, Clinton concentrated on rebuilding the U.S. economy. He achieved one of his major foreign policy goals in 1993 when Congress approved the North American Free Trade Agreement (NAFTA), which ended trade barriers between the United States, Mexico, and Canada. By Clinton's second term, the health of the country's economy was the best it had been in years. In 1994, Congress passed his anticrime bill. He also appointed more women and minorities to his cabinet than had any previous president. He was elected for a second term in 1996.

Advice for Chelsea

Patti Davis, former president Ronald Reagan's daughter, sent Chelsea some tips on coping with life as a White House kid. She said, "Get your own refrigerator for your bedroom because they don't keep food in the upstairs kitchen. Don't run off and leave your Secret Servicemen; it just makes them angry. Find the secret passageways in the White House and use them to hide out sometimes. Never pay attention to *anything* that anybody writes about you. Above all, keep a sense of humor."

As First Lady, Hillary Rodham Clinton says she has loved the challenges of the White House. Instead of limiting herself to one project, she has pushed for better health care for all Americans, worked for the welfare of single moms and their children, and acted as her husband's emissary around the world.

Chelsea Clinton was only twelve years old when her father became president. Although her parents had tried to prepare her for the experience, it was reported that Chelsea burst into tears when she heard her father had been elected. She was happy for him, but she was scared about such a big move. Her black-and-white cat, Socks, made her feel more at home, but both Chelsea's parents are allergic to him.

When Bill became president, he and Hillary told the press that they intended to keep Chelsea's life as normal and private as possible. To date, the press has largely respected Chelsea's privacy.

In December 1997, a new pet came to join Socks. The president got a three-month-old Labrador retriever. He named the dog Buddy after a beloved great-uncle who had died several months before. When the big, gangling puppy was introduced to the press, Clinton's face was wreathed in smiles and he seemed as thrilled as a little kid over his new dog. Buddy was all over the place, pulling the president around the White House Rose Garden. The new arrival was soon on his way to obedience school to learn how to be First Dog!

During his political career and as our sitting president, William Jefferson Clinton has been very successful, yet he has suffered many attacks, defeats, and setbacks. Midway into his second term, the House of Representatives impeached President Clinton, bringing charges that he committed perjury (lied under oath) and obstructed justice by not disclosing his personal relationship with a White House intern, Monica Lewinsky, when he testified in the Paula Jones civil case. Following a trial in the U.S. Senate, the president was acquitted. He remains one of the most popular presidents in history.

☆ Visit the ☆ CLINTON Home

Bill Clinton's birthplace, where he lived with his maternal grandparents during the first four years of his life, has been restored and placed on the National Register of Historic Sites and is open to the public.

The two-and-one-half-story American foursquare house in Clinton's hometown of Hope, Arkansas, was built in 1917. When restoration began in 1993, it had not been owned by members of Clinton's family for over thirty years and in that time, the house had suffered fire, water, and structural damage. (During the restoration of the house, the president's late mother, Virginia Kelley, was personally involved in providing details that would bring the place back to its 1946 appearance when it belonged to her parents.)

The Clinton Home is located at 117 South Hervey Street in Hope, Arkansas, 35 miles south of Texarkana. Open Tuesday through Saturday, 10 A.M. to 4:30 P.M., Sunday 1 P.M. to 5 P.M. during the spring and summer, and Tuesday through Saturday, 10 A.M. to 4:30 P.M. during the fall and winter. Adults $5, senior citizens $4, children under 6 free. Children 6–18, military, and tours $3. For more information: Clinton Birthplace Foundation, P.O. Box 1925, Hope, AK 71802. Telephone: 870-777-4455. Web Site: http://www.clintonbirthplace.com

Visit the WHITE HOUSE

Although it is the president's home and office, the White House is also a museum of American history, filled with priceless treasures that include some of America's finest paintings, antiques, and historic memorabilia. It is the only official residence of a head of state that is regularly open to the public free of charge. Over a million people a year tour the public rooms, while vital government business is being conducted in other rooms of the mansion.

Each tour begins in the wood-paneled East Wing lobby and continues along the wide ground floor corridor with its portraits of the First Ladies. Then you go up to the wide marble stairs and through the elegant rooms of the State Floor: the East Room, with its full-length portrait of George Washington; the Green Room, which is a first-floor parlor; the Blue Room, now used as a reception area; the Red Room, whose vivid walls set off a stunning portrait of Dolley Madison; and the elegant State Dining Room that can seat 140 guests. Tours end in the North Entrance, a beautiful area with a grand staircase, cut-glass chandeliers, marble floors, and bold red carpet.

The White House is located at 1600 Pennsylvania Avenue, between 15th and 16th Streets. From mid-March through early September, complimentary tickets are necessary and are given on a first-come, first-serve basis. Tickets can be obtained at the White House Visitor Center, 1450 Pennsylvania Avenue South, NW. Tours are given year-round Tuesday through Saturday from 10 A.M. to noon. Allow an hour to enjoy the White House. For more information: White House Visitors Tours, 1600 Pennsylvania Avenue, Washington, DC 20500. Telephone: 202-456-7041. Web site: http://www.whitehouse.gov/WH/welcome.html

Suggested Reading

Connelly, Thomas L. *Almanac of American Presidents.* New York, London: Facts On File, 1991.

Freedman, Russell. *Lincoln.* New York: Clarion Books, Ticknor & Fields, 1987.

LaVere, Anderson. *Tad Lincoln.* Champaign, IL: Garrad Publishing Co., 1971.

Meltzer, Milton. *George Washington and the Birth of Our Nation.* New York: Franklin Watts, 1986.

Nelson, Roy. *Wooden Teeth and Jelly Beans.* New York: Scholastic Press, 1995.

Radcliffe, Donnie. *Hillary Rodham Clinton.* New York: Warner Books, 1993.

Rubel, David. *Scholastic Encyclopedia of the Presidents and Their Times.* New York: Scholastic Press, 1994.

Smithsonian Exposition Books. *Every Four Years.* New York: W. W. Norton & Co., 1980.

Whitney, Dan C. *American Presidents,* 7th edition. New York: Prentice Hall, 1990.

Zeman, Anne, and Kate Kelly. *Everything You Need to Know About American History Homework.* New York: Scholastic Press. Revised edition 1997.